CENSORSHIP

and

Selection

Issues and Answers for Schools

A joint publication of

American Library Association
Chicago and London

American Association of School Administrators
Arlington, Virginia

1993

This publication can be purchased from the

American Library Association
50 East Huron Street, Chicago, Illinois 60611
Phone: 312/944-6780
ISBN: 0-8389-0620-6

or from the

American Association of School Administrators
1801 North Moore Street, Arlington, Virginia 22209
Phone: 703/528-0700
ISBN: 0-87652-197-9
AASA Stock Number: 021-00219

Managing Editor: Kay Solt
Composed by Publishing Services, Inc.,
  in Caslon 224 on Xyvision/Cg8600
Printed on 50-pound Glatfelter, a pH-neutral stock,
  and bound in 10-point C1S cover stock
  by Edwards Brothers, Inc.

Library of Congress Cataloging-in-Publication Data
Reichman, Henry, 1947–
  Censorship and selection : issues and answers for schools / by
Henry Reichman.—Rev. ed.
    p.   cm.
  Includes bibliographical references.
    1. School libraries—Censorship—United States.   2. Book
selection—United States.   3. School libraries—Collection
development—United States.   4. Teaching, Freedom of—United States.
5. Education—Curricula—Censorship—United States.   6. Freedom of
the press—United States.   7. Student publications—Censorship—
United States.   8. Children's literature—Censorship—United
States.   I. Title.
Z675.S3R42   1993
025.2'1878'0973—dc20   93-19711

Printed in the United States of America.

97 96 95 94 93   5 4 3 2 1

Points of view or opinions in this book are those of the author and do not
necessarily represent the official positions, beliefs, or policies of the American
Library Association or the American Association of School Administrators.

CONTENTS

Preface, vii

Acknowledgments, ix

Chapter 1—Censorship in the Schools, 1

What Is Censorship?
Censorship and Education
Censorship or Selection?
Academic Freedom
The Extent of the Problem
Who Censors?
Motives for Censorship
Self-Censorship

Chapter 2—Arenas of Conflict, 21

The School Library and the Library Bill of Rights
The School Library: Selection Policies
The Classroom
The Student Press

Chapter 3—Issues in Dispute, 33

Politics
"Global Education"
"Dirty" Words
Profanity and Policy
Sexuality
Gay and Lesbian Literature
Sex Education
Violence
"Secular Humanism" and "New Age"
Witchcraft and the Occult
The *Impressions* Controversy
Creationism
Racism and Sexism
The Case of Huck Finn

Chapter 4—Establishing Selection Policies, 61

Who Makes Policy?
Basic Components of a Selection Policy
Objectives
Responsibility for Selection
Criteria
Procedures
Controversial Materials
Reconsideration
The Completed Policy
Student Rights and the Student Press

Chapter 5—What Do We Do If . . . ?, 76

Some General Rules
Preparing for A Crisis
Handling the Initial Complaint
The Reconsideration Committee
If They Won't "Play by the Rules"
If "The Community Is Up In Arms"
If the Challenge Succeeds

Chapter 6—What Is The Law?, 88

Basic Principles
Differing Views and Unresolved Issues
School Libraries: The *Pico* Decision
The Lower Courts: An Ambiguous Record
Religion in the Schools
Evolution and Creation
Student Rights and Student Press
Library and Curricular Censorship After *Hazelwood*

Chapter 7—School System Checklist, 106

Preparation
Response

Chapter 8—Conclusion, 110

Appendixes, 113

A   Access to Resources and Services in the School Library Media Program

B   Free Access to Libraries for Minors

C   Diversity in Collection Development

D   Tips and Samples for Writing a Selection Policy

E   Sample Letter to Complainant

F   Sample Instructions to Evaluating Committee

G   Sample Statement of Concern about Library/Media Center Resources

H   Guidelines for Student Publications

I   Tips for Dealing with Concerns about Library Resources

J   Selected List of Concerned National Organizations

K   Summaries of Selcted Legal Cases

L   A Selected, Annotated Bibliography on the First Amendment and Intellectual Freedom

Notes, 165

PREFACE

"Censorship!" The word itself sparks debate—even more so when the context is the public school. In recent years complaints about school library materials, textbooks, and other educational resources have plunged teachers, parents, administrators, and school boards, in big cities and suburbs, rural areas and larger towns, in all regions of the country, into controversy and turmoil. Whether the issue is "dirty words," "traditional values," or racial insensitivity, censorship unchallenged threatens the very fabric of public education.

The American Library Association and the American Association of School Administrators have worked together for many years to address issues surrounding public school censorship and academic freedom. This timely revision of *Censorship and Selection* continues our efforts to provide educators and citizens alike with information essential to sustaining the free marketplace of ideas in education.

In its first edition, published in 1988, *Censorship and Selection* won broad praise not only as the most thorough survey available of the school censorship controversy, but as the only work to offer educators concrete and practical advice on how to prepare selection policies, handle complaints, and meet challenges. Covering the student press as well as library and curricular materials, the book has proven an indispensable guide for both strife-torn school districts and those seeking to avoid destructive conflicts. This updated and expanded edition includes new material on the "hot" censorship disputes of the '90s, including challenges to gay and lesbian literature and allegedly occult materials. The chapter on the legal environment has been expanded to discuss cases decided since 1987, and offers a thorough treatment of the impact of the U.S. Supreme Court's landmark *Hazelwood* student press ruling.

Censorship and Selection remains essential reading for anyone who cares deeply about the preservation of a free and democratic society based on openness.

Gary Marx
Executive Director
American Association
   of School Administrators

Judith F. Krug
Director
Office for Intellectual Freedom
American Library Association

ACKNOWLEDGMENTS

Like its predecessor, the revised edition of *Censorship and Selection: Issues and Answers for Schools* is a joint publication of the American Library Association and the American Association of School Administrators, two national organizations that are steadfastly committed to the principles and maintenance of intellectual freedom, which is the basis for our free and democratic society.

Its publication would not have been possible without the foresight of ALA and AASA staff and the efforts of its talented author, Henry Reichman. Judith Krug, Director of the Office for Intellectual Freedom at the ALA and Gary Marx, Executive Director for Communications at the AASA, reviewed the revision. In his updating, Reichman drew upon his work as Associate Editor and principal writer of the American Library Association's *Newsletter on Intellectual Freedom,* as well as on his longtime interest and research in political and social movements in the United States, the former Soviet Union, and elsewhere. Special thanks go to the readers of this manuscript and of the *Newsletter* for sharing information and ideas on this important subject.

ACKNOWLEDGEMENTS

Censorship in the Schools

It can hardly be argued that either students or teachers shed their constitutional rights to freedom of speech or expression at the schoolhouse gate. . . . In our system, students may not be regarded as closed-circuit recipients of only that which the State chooses to communicate.

Tinker v. Des Moines Independent Community School District[1]

For educators, the past decade has been a time of controversy and, occasionally, fear. A growing and sometimes acrimonious debate over the proper role and function of public education in a free society has frequently placed teachers, librarians, and school administrators in a difficult position. Curricular changes are demanded from every quarter; methods of instruction have come under intense scrutiny; teacher shortages are predicted, while the competence of existing personnel is challenged—all amid an increasingly somber fiscal atmosphere.

From one side, we hear that standards have fallen, that too often schools do not leave their graduates with a grasp of even the most basic skills needed for survival in the modern world. From another side, we are told that students are given too much, that schools teach things best left unlearned, or—at the least—subjects better treated in the home by parents. For some, the problem is sex education: there is too much of it or, perhaps, not enough. For others, the concern is religion—from prayer in school to the teaching of evolution or even, as increasing numbers allege, of witchcraft and the occult.

There is fear among many that, in seeking to avoid public entanglement with private religion, our schools fail to instill in students the kinds of educational and moral values shared by Americans of all faiths. Some even charge that public education has come to promote its own religious doctrines—so-called "secular humanism" or, more commonly in recent years, "New Age" and Satanism. One Florida couple told their school board that "all the evils of society are nurtured by the books available" in schools.[2]

The debate over education is and should be ongoing and constructive. It is, after all, a debate about the future, about the fate of our most precious resource, our children. As in all discussion of complex issues, no one may claim a monopoly on truth. Valuable insights have come from advocates of virtually every philosophy. Welcome initiatives have been proposed by a wide variety of social, professional, and political groups. But it is precisely the wide-ranging and diverse character of our national discussion of education that gives rise to a growing concern about censorship. For ultimately, ideas proposed become actions taken.

Although most participants in the debate over education respect the rights and sincerity of their opponents, some have sought to impose their views on the educational system, not through processes of persuasion and compromise, but by attempting to remove or restrict the use of certain instructional and library materials. A few have also called into question the processes by which these materials are selected, often demanding a special or expanded role for themselves or for others with similar convictions. Whether it is parents, clergy, educators, or agents of government who take action, efforts to impose on our schools a single political, religious, or moral agenda threaten to foreclose debate and cripple education.

What Is Censorship?

Put briefly, censorship is the removal, suppression, or restricted circulation of literary, artistic, or educational materials—of images, ideas, and information—on the grounds that these are morally or otherwise objectionable in light of standards applied by the censor. Frequently, the single occurrence of an offending word will arouse protest. In other cases, objection will be made to the underlying values and basic message conveyed—or said to be conveyed—by a given work. In the final analysis, censorship is simply a matter of someone saying: "No, you cannot read that magazine or book or see that film or videotape—because I don't like it." According to some, only agents of government may censor. Yet, in reality, pressures exerted by private citizens or citizen groups can also result in removal or suppression of "objectionable" items. In such situations these private individuals and groups function as true and effective censors.

Pressures to remove allegedly "offensive" classroom or school library materials have attracted considerable media attention. Typically, individual parents or parent/citizen groups bring some kind of pressure upon school boards or administrators, who in turn might tell librarians not to circulate, or teachers not to assign, a challenged work. More often than not, school systems resist such pressure. In some cases, however, professional educators or school boards have initiated removal or restriction. In other instances, teachers, librarians, and school principals acceded to censorship pressures, but were reversed by higher-level administrators or school boards. In March 1987, for the first time in U.S. history, a federal court took on the role of school book censor when a Mobile, Alabama, judge ordered public school districts in that state to remove from classrooms 44 state-approved social studies, history, and home economics textbooks because they allegedly promote "secular humanism," a violation, the judge ruled, of the constitutional separation of church and state. Fortunately, the U.S. Court of Appeals reversed that decision in August 1987.

That instance notwithstanding, the courts have tended to give local school districts wide discretion in determining what they will teach and with which materials. In the 1968 case of *Epperson v. Arkansas*, the U.S. Supreme Court declared: "Public education in our Nation is committed to the control of state and local authorities. Courts do not and cannot intervene in the resolution of conflicts which arise in the daily operation of school systems and which do not directly and sharply implicate basic constitutional values."[3]

Still, in *Epperson*, the Supreme Court struck down a state law that prohibited the teaching of evolution. Court decisions give school authorities broad discretion in making educational decisions, but not judgments that smack of ideological, political, or religious motivations. The Supreme Court has frequently upheld the overriding importance of free expression. The First Amendment, the Court declared in 1976, "does not tolerate laws which cast a pall of orthodoxy over the classroom . . . students must always remain free to inquire, to study and to evaluate, to gain new maturity and understanding."[4] In 1982, the Supreme Court ruled, in a plurality opinion written by Justice William J. Brennan, Jr., that "local school boards may not remove books from school library shelves simply because they dislike the ideas contained in those books and seek by their removal to prescribe what shall be orthodox in politics, nationalism, religion, or other matters of opinion."[5]

Although censors almost invariably claim to be defending American values, educational censorship is harmful precisely because it undermines those very democratic values of tolerance and intellectual freedom that our educational system must seek to instill. In the process of acquiring knowledge and searching for truth, students learn to discriminate and choose—to make decisions rationally and logically in light of evidence. Removing a book from a classroom or school library because it offends some members of the community increases the likelihood that students will see suppression as an acceptable way of responding to controversial ideas and images.

By suppressing materials containing ideas or themes with which they do not agree, censors produce a sterile conformity and a lack of intellectual and emotional growth in students. Freedom in the public schools is central to the quality of what and how students learn.

Censorship and Education

Americans find censorship odious. Few in our society advocate the banning of all but a tiny handful of materials from sale, circulation, or display to adults. The commitment to free expression is not so clear, however, where minors are concerned, and the picture becomes more clouded still when the issue of schooling enters. The power to choose some textbooks or library materials and to reject others according to standards appropriate to education's inculcative mission is central to the schooling enterprise. The purpose of education is not only to communicate factual information, but to develop in the young the ability to discriminate and choose. This, of necessity, involves some selective transmission of values.

As legal scholar Mark Yudof has noted:

> ... indoctrination is much of what schools are about. But it is not all that schools are about. If government is to educate children, to operate public schools, and to select teachers, books and courses, a basic decision has been made about the communication of skills, attitudes, values, and beliefs between generations. Education and indoctrination, information and values, cannot be neatly disentangled.... And this learning is not value neutral.
>
> The problem, however, lies in devising educational systems that prepare children for adult life without simultaneously sacrificing their ability to reflect upon the ends for which they are being prepared, without indoctrinating them to unbridled allegiance to the *status quo* or to the rightness of current institutional arrangements.... Education can expand the mind and imagination or contract them. The child who is taught nothing of his or her country's cultural, political, and intellectual heritage must be pitied as much as the child who is compelled to conform in all respects to the conventional wisdom.[6]

The question then becomes: Who determines what is to be taught in the public schools and how? Who takes charge of the necessary balancing between education and socialization, between the communication of diverse ideas and the inculcation of common values?

In our country, this power is generally vested in elected representatives of the voters—school board members—whose actions are constrained, however, by broad constitutional and customary limits, and who most frequently delegate their authority to professional administrators and educators. But the matter is not really that simple. Teachers and librarians claim special wisdom in determining curriculum by virtue of their training and experience. They may demand additional rights to academic freedom and to reasonable autonomy in carrying out professional responsibilities. Parents, too, have an important interest in directing the upbringing of their children, and may justifiably demand influence over the curriculum beyond the power they wield together with nonparents as voters. Students themselves have also, not unreasonably, asserted rights to know, to read, to learn, and not to be subjected to materials they find offensive.

When any of these groups object to certain educational materials, may they fairly be branded censors? Many say no. They charge that it is frequently the schools themselves that censor materials according to the views of the educational "establishment." Some critics of education assert that schools may use their governmentally granted powers to indoctrinate students in ways that undermine the ability to think and act critically, or that subvert popular values which, for whatever reason, the state or its agents fear. The Florida textbook critics cited earlier told their school board that objectionable "books are forced on you because they are approved by the federal government and the state of Florida."[7] As Yudof points out, "The government's capacity to shape beliefs and attitudes may be as destructive of democratic values as direct censorship."[8]

Censorship or Selection?

Objections made by parents and others to school classroom and library materials must be seen, then, as an important and valuable part of the democratic and educational process. Although many, if not most, challenges to such materials do amount to little more than censorship attempts—and should therefore be rejected—the challenge process itself is a legitimate and very important avenue of communication.

Legitimate constraints on intellectual freedom in education are not always easily distinguished from those that are improper. Nevertheless, a distinction can and must be made between selection and censorship. Intelligent selection of educational materials is by no means an easy task. The interests and opinions of a wide variety of groups need to be balanced, and it is likely that charges of censorship or bias will be hurled at even the most diligent school system. Still, clearly articulated and professionally formulated selection policies and procedures differ fundamentally from the mode of operation of the censor.

In general, selection is carried out by trained professionals, familiar with the wide variety of available choices and guided by a clear grasp of the educational purposes to be fulfilled. To be sure, the professional educator also has opinions, viewpoints, and values. One purpose of professional training, however, is to develop the ability to recognize and transcend personal bias. The professional should also know how to take into account and work with community and parental concerns, while still maintaining a high tolerance for our national diversity. By contrast, the censor's judgment is that of the individual, and it is most frequently based on criteria that are inherently personal and often intolerant.

Where the censor seeks reasons to *exclude* materials, those engaged in the process of selection look for ways to *include* the widest possible variety of textbooks, library materials, and curricular supplements within the context of a well-defined curriculum with clearly articulated goals. Censorship responds to diversity with suppression; the selection process seeks instead to familiarize students with the breadth of available images and information, while simultaneously erecting essential guideposts for the development of truly independent thought.

Academic Freedom

"Academic freedom is the freedom to teach and to learn. In defending the freedom to teach and to learn, we affirm the democratic process itself."

These are the opening lines of "Free to Learn: A Policy on Academic Freedom and Public Education" adopted by the Connecticut State Board of Education in 1981. In a similar vein, the Minnesota State Board of Education declared in 1985 that "The freedom to teach, to learn, and to express ideas without fear of censorship are fundamental rights held by public school teachers and students . . ."[9]

Respect for academic freedom is a hallowed tradition in American education. Academic freedom is generally understood to guarantee the teacher's right to teach and to select classroom materials, and the librarian's right to build an appropriate collection, according to established policies and procedures, without external interference. But few would deny that this freedom has its limits, and that it means different things in different situations.

Robert M. O'Neil, Director of the Thomas Jefferson Center for the Protection of Free Expression and formerly president of the Universities of Wisconsin and Virginia, has remarked: "Even the most ardent teacher-rights proponent would probably agree that elementary and secondary school instructors are not exactly like university professors, and that some dimensions of academic freedom diminish as one moves from graduate school to the younger grades."[10]

Academic freedom has also come to embrace the student's rights to learn and to expression. As the U.S. Supreme Court ruled in 1969:

> School officials do not possess absolute authority over their students. Students in school as well as out of school are "persons" under our Constitution. They are possessed of fundamental rights which the State must respect, just as they themselves must respect their obligations to the State.[11]

In particular, the courts have found that student publications, official and underground, enjoy broad—though not unfettered—protection against censorship. Still, a student's right to learn generally does not include the right to choose his or her own textbooks, or to demand the teaching of specialized subjects. Student expressional rights are also constrained by the school's interest in avoiding material and substantial disruptions of school activities.

Limits on academic freedom may vary according to the subject matter. A high school English teacher formulating a syllabus for an advanced placement course may have wide latitude to choose provocative and important works of literature, while an earth science teacher in the same school is not free to select a text advocating a "flat earth" theory. An elementary school librarian needs freedom to select books that appeal to a variety of conflicting tastes, but a classroom teacher may be constrained to use a reading text from a standardized series used in all elementary grades.

In general, as the distinction increasingly has been made between required texts and set curricula on the one hand, and collateral materials and a flexible curriculum on the other, the freedom and responsibility of teachers and librarians have grown. Expanded and diversified curricula have tended to enhance the role of teachers and school librarians in the selection of instructional materials.

A survey of high school curricula in 1894 found that no more than 40 separate subjects were taught. By 1950, the number of subjects taught in the same communities had risen to 274. A 1972 survey of Ohio schools revealed that of 392 schools responding, 65 offered electives in literature. A more recent national survey showed that more than a thousand literature courses are being offered in American high schools.[12]

The purposes of censorship may be accomplished without the removal or restriction of specific materials, but through the power to more broadly limit curricula. As O'Neil concludes:

> An elected school board does enjoy substantial latitude in setting the curriculum and in changing it. If a district chooses to offer only basic subjects, teachers in that district will enjoy quite limited freedom of expression. If, on the other hand, the school board decides to enrich the curriculum by offering advanced courses in drama, literature, government, and other complex and possibly controversial subjects, it must bear the consequences. Instructors hired to teach such courses properly enjoy a measure of intellectual freedom not available to their colleagues in manual training, home economics, and typing.[13]

In Warsaw, Indiana, in 1977, the school board conducted a curriculum review which resulted in the discontinuance of certain courses, as well as the removal of some books, the dismissal of several teachers, and the discontinuance of publication of the high school newspaper. The board's transparent motive in canceling courses in Black Literature, Gothic Literature, Folklore and Legend, and Science Fiction was to respond to objections made by some parents and board members against allegedly salacious or otherwise "objectionable" books used in those classes.

Whether or not elementary and secondary school teachers enjoy academic freedom comparable to that of college faculty, most experts believe that they, like librarians, should be left largely free to exercise professional judgment in selecting materials and determining how a course is to be taught. A report by a commission of the American Association of University Professors declared:

> Uncertainty as to whether any particular instructional material may be suppressed can only inhibit teachers and librarians in the exercise of their professional judgment.... And if teachers and librarians cannot exercise their professional judgment as to what is educationally sound, within the legitimate constraints imposed by the schools, then the way is

open for outside pressure groups to determine the limits of unobjection-
able discourse in the schools.[14]

Students learn how to think independently from their teachers—not only
through instruction but also, and perhaps more directly, through example.
As the famed legal scholar and civil liberties activist Alexander Meiklejohn
said, "To require our teachers to say to their pupils, 'I want you to learn
from me how to do what I am forbidden to do,' is to make of education the
most utter nonsense."[15]

The Extent of the Problem

How big a problem is censorship in our public schools? No one can say
for certain, since there is little agreement about how to measure the
phenomenon and no one has yet funded a large enough and fully
scientific survey. Still, there is almost universal agreement that, to
quote a 1980 report, the problem is "real, nationwide, and growing."

In March 1986, a report to the U.S. Senate Subcommittee on Ap-
propriations for the Departments of Labor, Health and Human
Services, and Education and Related Agencies, prepared by the U.S.
National Commission on Libraries and Information Science (NCLIS)
reached the following conclusions:[16]

- After a decrease between 1975 and 1979, attempts to remove, restrict, or alter public school library materials increased dramatically,
  reaching a peak in 1982. Since 1983, the numbers have remained
  roughly constant, although at a level higher than at any time since
  1975.
- Challenges were reported from all regions of the country and from
  urban, suburban, and rural locations. Challenged publications included materials for all grade levels.
- As recently as a decade ago, almost no case law existed in the area of
  library censorship. Now there is a substantial and growing body of
  case law on public school library censorship attempts, reflecting a
  dramatic increase in litigation and, presumably, in this sort of activity.

People for the American Way, a public interest group, has released
ten annual reports on the censorship of public school library and
curricular materials under the title, *Attacks on the Freedom to Learn*.
These reveal a steady increase in the number of reported censorship
incidents. Over the report's initial five years, the number of incidents
recorded rose by 168 percent. Between school years 1987–88 and

1988–89 the number of reported incidents rose again, by approximately 10 percent, and another 40 percent increase was recorded in 1989–90. In 1990–91, the report cited 229 instances of attempted censorship in 45 states, a 20 percent increase that made it "the single worst year for school censorship in the history of our research," according to Arthur J. Kropp, the organization's president. "The 1990s are taking shape as the decade of the censor, and the public schools have not been spared," Kropp told reporters.

That prediction seemed to be confirmed when, a year later, the 1991–92 report documented 376 incidents in 44 states, a whopping increase of 64 percent in a single year. The report said there were 348 cases in which organizations or individuals tried to remove or restrict the use of literature, instructional materials, activities, or programs in classrooms and school libraries. Twenty-eight related episodes involved ideological pressure upon schools, without specific materials being targeted.

According to *Attacks on the Freedom to Learn, 1991–92*, in 144 incidents, or 41 percent of the cases, challenges to library books and curricula actually led to removal or restriction of challenged materials. Ten years earlier, only 23 percent of the reported challenges were successful. In recent years, the report has revealed a significant shift in the nature of the attacks. Where previous critics tended to target so-called "dirty books" in school libraries, would-be censors now more frequently object to instructional materials and methods. Still, of the 229 incidents reported in the 1990–91 report, 72 (31 percent) were to works that no child was required to read—books in libraries and on optional reading lists. In another 41 cases (18 percent) teachers suggested alternate assignments, but challengers were not satisfied.[17]

These studies were based on publicly reported incidents, however, which may tend to skew the results according to how much attention the media are paying to the issue. The NCLIS report estimated that only about 15 percent of all school censorship efforts are reported in the media. However, surveys conducted by a variety of organizations tend to confirm the conclusions of media-based reports.

An extensive national survey of the problem was conducted in 1980 by the Association of American Publishers (AAP), the American Library Association (ALA), and the Association for Supervision and Curriculum Development (ASCD). Responses to a 52–item questionnaire were received from 1,891 school principals, librarians, and district superintendents from all 50 states and the District of Columbia. These were supplemented by a separate survey of and extensive interviews with state-level adoption officials in 20 of the 22 states having statewide textbook adoption procedures. The survey report concluded without qualification that "challenges to instructional and library materials in the public schools occur in all regions of the country and in all types of communities, and that such pressures are increasing."[18]

The report revealed several disturbing trends:

- Challenges to materials by survey respondents "sought, *overwhelmingly*, to *limit* rather than *expand* the materials available to students." (emphasis in original) More than half of all reported challenges to instructional or library materials resulted in either their removal or some other limitation on access or use.
- Library materials were reported challenged significantly more often than classroom materials, and were more frequently removed or restricted as a result. Perhaps one of the most startling findings of the survey was that librarians named school personnel as initiating more than 30 percent of the incidents reported.
- Approximately half of the objections raised were to isolated passages or features of the material (representation of sexual relations, "dirty words," and the like), rather than to the ideas in or the ideological nature of the work taken as a whole. In fact, about one in three challengers readily admitted to not having examined the material in full. Nor, in most cases, had the school communicated reasons for using the material, suggesting that challenges were often made without consideration of the challenged work's overall educational value.
- In half of the incidents reported, the challenged material was subjected to some degree of restriction or censorship *prior to formal review*. The majority of challenges were dealt with informally, rather than according to established policies and through structured procedures. In nearly half the reported cases, no one was assigned to reevaluate the challenged material.

Under the sponsorship of the National Council of Teachers of English, Professor Lee Burress of the University of Wisconsin surveyed several thousand high school librarians in small, medium-sized, and large schools in 1966, 1973, 1977, and 1982. He found a steady increase in the reported number of censorship incidents and in the perception of censorship pressures by school librarians. He also discovered a significant increase in the percentage of challenges made by organized community groups rather than individuals, up from just 1 percent of all challenges in 1966 to 17 percent in 1982. Professor Burress has compiled a list of 836 book titles against which objections have been made, including many well-known classics.[19]

In 1990, with support from the U.S. Department of Education and Encyclopaedia Britannica, Professor Dianne McAfee Hopkins of the University of Wisconsin-Madison School of Library and Information Studies surveyed over 6,500 public secondary school libraries and media centers, of which 72 percent responded. Of this group, 1,661, more than a third, reported one or more challenges to library or media center materials between 1986 and 1989. In nearly half these incidents the challenged materials were either removed or access to them was restricted.[20]

These findings are consistent with the results of a small, informal survey of school districts conducted specifically for the first edition of this book by the American Association of School Administrators (AASA) in June 1987. Of the 215 school districts responding, 77 (or 36 percent) reported a total of more than 200 challenges to instructional or library materials since June 1982. Among all districts responding, 10 percent described the number of challenges as *greater* than five years before, 8 percent as *fewer* than five years before, and about half said the number was about the same, with the remaining respondents uncertain. Among those reporting incidents, however, about one in four said that challenges had increased in number, while only four of these districts reported a decline in such activity.

Of the 77 districts reporting challenges to materials, 10 reported the removal of instructional items, another 10 reported changes in classroom materials, and 20 reported the removal of books or other materials from libraries and media centers.

One perception common among educators and the general public is that the problem of book censorship is confined to—or, at least, worst in—the South, especially those regions considered part of the "Bible Belt." According to a 1985 survey of librarians in four southern states— Alabama, Georgia, Louisiana, and Tennessee—conducted by the American Civil Liberties Union, 30.9 percent of public school libraries in those states had been targets of attempts to restrict access to or to remove materials since 1980. Of the 290 challenges to school library materials reported, the material in question was removed from the library 36.8 percent of the time.[21] Survey studies of teachers in North Carolina in 1989 and Florida in 1990 revealed that more than a quarter of those responding to each survey had experienced a censorship challenge within the past few years.[22] In 1991–92, the People for the American Way report recorded more incidents in Florida than any other state, due largely to twenty separate instances in the city of Jacksonville alone.[23] Another study of school librarians in half of Virginia's public schools found that one in three libraries experienced censorship pressures between 1979 and 1982.[24]

However, as Arthur J. Kropp of People for the American Way has emphasized, "The notion that it's a redneck, rural problem is a myth."[25] His group's 1991–92 report documented incidents in 44 states and every region of the country, with the midwestern states the most active, with 119 incidents. The northeast region had the fewest challenges, with 59 incidents. In the previous year's report, the western region reported 85 incidents; the Midwest 70 incidents; the South 63 incidents; and the Northeast 46 incidents.[26]

A 1983 survey in Minnesota revealed that 90 of 244 secondary school libraries (36.8 percent), and 70 of 149 elementary school libraries (47.0 percent) had experienced challenges. In secondary schools, materials were removed or restricted in 36 percent of cases; in elementary schools, 33 percent. A follow-up survey completed eight years later revealed little change, with challenges reported by 39 percent of all school libraries responding.[27] An Ohio survey found 21 percent of school librarians responding that they had censorship problems, with "objectionable" materials removed in 45 percent of the cases, and restricted to closed shelves in 17 percent.[28] In Oregon, the state's Intellectual Freedom Clearinghouse has conducted four annual surveys of school library censorship since the 1987–88 school year, with fluctuating results. In 1987–88, Oregon school libraries reported 7 challenges. This tripled to 21 the following year, but dropped to 9 in 1989–90. In 1990–91, the number of challenges reported was again 21.[29]

In June 1989, the Missouri Coalition Against Censorship reported the results of a survey of more than 500 school districts throughout the state. More than half of the thirty percent of the districts responding reported censorship attempts during the previous two years, of which 53 percent succeeded. Put more bluntly, more than one of every four districts in Missouri had material removed, restricted, or otherwise made unavailable for use by students or teachers between 1987 and 1989. In another 1989 survey, 23 percent of Vermont school librarians reported censorship incidents.[30]

Given that one in eight Americans lives in California, it is hardly surprising that the state has experienced the most incidents of censorship. In 1990–91, People for the American Way reported 36 incidents in California. Oregon was the second most active state with 19 incidents, followed by Michigan with 17, Illinois with 15, and Texas with 13.[31] But according to a 1990 survey conducted by a professor at California State University, Fullerton, under the auspices of the Educational Congress of California, the problem in the Golden State is even worse than these figures would suggest. More than 40 percent of California's school districts responded to this survey with 35.6 percent reporting more than 300 challenges over a two-year period. Only about a fourth of the reported challenges were covered by local, state, or national media.[32]

Who Censors?

Almost anything can be a target of censorship. According to People for the American Way's 1990–91 report, "Challenges were registered against classic works of literature, sex-education programs, a "nuclear peace" program, AIDS prevention and drug abuse prevention curricula, biology instruction, self-esteem development projects, guidance counseling programs, and a range of other materials." The most frequently challenged title was a popular reading series, *Impressions* (see chapters 2 and 3), but the list of heavily censored titles also included old standbys like J. D. Salinger's *The Catcher in the Rye* and acknowledged classics like *The Grapes of Wrath* and *The Adventures of Huckleberry Finn.*[33]

Over the past two decades, probably the most challenged author has been juvenile and young adult writer Judy Blume. Young adult authors Robert Cormier and Norma Klein are also frequent targets of protest. But the list of challenged material includes many works by distinguished adult writers, such as Nobel or Pulitzer Prize winners Saul Bellow, William Golding, John Steinbeck, Alice Walker, John Updike, and Norman Mailer, as well as classic works by authors like William Shakespeare, Mark Twain, and Vladimir Nabokov. In 1987, censorship pressures in a Florida district led a school superintendent to ban 63 different titles requested by high school teachers for instructional use, including several Shakespeare plays, *The Red Badge of Courage, The Great Gatsby,* and works by Ernest Hemingway, Eugene O'Neill, and others.[34]

Who would object to such works and what motivates them? Chapter 3 will discuss some of the major issues around which controversy has developed and examine some typical and recent instances where objections have been raised. But here a few general observations about the impulse to censor are in order.

The word "censor" often evokes the mental picture of an irrational, belligerent individual. In most instances, however, it is a sincerely concerned parent or citizen interested in the future of education who complains about curricular or library materials. Complainants may not have a broad knowledge of literature or of the principles of intellectual freedom, but their motives in questioning the use of educational materials are seldom unusual. Complainants may honestly believe that certain materials will corrupt children and adolescents, offend the sensitive or unwary reader, or undermine basic values and beliefs.

Over the past decade a number of national, regional, and local political or religious organizations have emerged that advocate the removal or restriction of library and classroom materials, usually as part of a broader program of educational reform. Increasingly, members of these organizations have sought and often won election to school and library boards. Whether such groups initiate censorship pressures or enter controversies already in progress, their presence often exacerbates tensions. The involvement of more organized and sometimes highly sophisticated political or religious groups—be they of a conservative Christian, minority rights or other orientation—in real or potential censorship conflicts certainly creates additional problems for besieged educators. Educators need to recall, however, that these groups act within their rights when they seek to participate in school government and in the debate over educational policy. It is not the role of this book to condemn or to praise any specific educational program, or any organization or tendency, but to mobilize opposition to the imposition of censorship by anyone, including those who have organized to express sincerely held political or religious views.

Although an attempt to stereotype the censor would be unfair, one generalization can be made: Regardless of specific motives, would-be censors share one belief: that they can recognize "evil" and that other people should be protected from it. Censors do not necessarily think their own morals need protection, but they do feel compelled to save their fellows, especially minors.

Professor John Wakefield of the University of North Alabama served on his state's textbook committee with an individual who, with the help of supporters, systematically sought the disapproval of teaching materials that violated his personal morality and religious faith. Wakefield's assessment of this individual also describes many other would-be censors:

> His flaw in thinking came from his apparent inability to entertain intellectual perspectives other than his own. At one crucial juncture . . . I asked him if it were not important to suspend judgment long enough to understand the position of another, and I was surprised by his resounding "No." He especially claimed that some prejudice always exists since suspension of judgment is theoretically impossible. He had a closed mind on some issues, and he was not interested in entertaining an intellectual view of what he considered to be exclusively moral matters.[35]

Motives for Censorship

Motivations for censorship may be grouped into four general catego-
ries.[36] These are by no means exclusive. Indeed, they often merge—
both in outward appearance and in the censor's mind. Underlying each
is often a profound fear and distrust of pluralism, and an unexpressed
(even unrecognized) desire to homogenize society to make others
more like the censor (or, more accurately, like the censor's self-image).

- **Family values.** A would-be censor may feel threatened by changes
  in accepted and traditional ways of life. Changes in attitudes toward the family and related customs are naturally reflected in
  library and classroom materials. Explicitly sexual works in particular are often viewed as obvious causes of repeated deviation from
  older norms. Some censors want to protect children from exposure
  to works dealing frankly with sexual topics and themes because
  these are perceived as a challenge to their values.
- **Political views.** Changes in political life can be equally threatening. The censor may view a work that is thought to advocate radical
  change as subversive or "un-American." If such works also contain
  less than polite language, it will not be difficult for the censor to
  mount an attack on the grounds of obscenity in addition to—and
  sometimes in order to disguise—objections on forthrightly political grounds.
- **Religion.** A potential censor may view explicitly sexual works and
  politically or socially unorthodox ideas as attacks on religious
  faith. Materials deemed damaging to religious beliefs cause concern about a society many see as growing increasingly hostile to
  religious training and buttress fears about that society's steady
  disintegration.
- **Minority rights.** Not all would-be censors seek to preserve traditional values. The conservative censor has been joined by groups
  that want their own special group values recognized. For example,
  ethnic minorities and women struggling against long-established
  stereotypes may want to reject materials that challenge their
  cause. And these groups, too, may use the devices of censorship.
  Well-meaning efforts to impose on educational materials new orthodoxies of what some have termed "political correctness" verge
  on censorship when they, too, seek to limit rather than expand the
  educational horizon.

Whatever the censor's motives, attempts to suppress certain educational materials may also stem from a confused understanding of the purposes of schooling. The censor recognizes the central importance of education in our society. But the censor may fail to see that schools fulfill their obligations to a diverse community by teaching students to tolerate, understand, and appreciate diversity. Would-be censors may think that it is the purpose of the schools to support certain values or causes, which are, of course, *their* values and *their* causes. Moreover, they tend to believe that those values and causes are best promoted by denying a forum to competing values and causes.

Self-Censorship

Adoption of sound selection policies and procedures and of a fair procedure for reconsideration of instructional and library materials is commonly viewed as the best defense schools have against censorship.[37] This is true, as long as it is understood that adoption of such policies and procedures by no means guarantees that challenges will not occur. Indeed, quite the opposite may be true. The AASA survey revealed that among districts reporting challenges, 72 percent had a formal written policy and set of procedures for the selection of library materials. Among those that did not report challenges, however, only 41 percent had such a policy and set of procedures. In the 1980 survey conducted by AAP, ALA, and ASCD, those without established policies and procedures also reported fewer challenges than those with policies and procedures.

One way to explain the difference is by noting that districts that have been targets of censorship efforts tend to learn from experience, and to adopt, revise, or update appropriate measures. But it should also be recognized that informal challenges resolved in ad hoc ways often go unreported. Where sound formal policies and procedures are lacking—or are not observed—censorship efforts may quietly succeed. In these types of situations, teachers, librarians, or administrators may accede to pressure without any "incident" being registered. Perhaps more ominously, school personnel may initiate removals on their own, either to deter perceived threats or to impose their own values and orthodoxies on the educational process. In some cases, potentially controversial materials simply are not acquired in the first place.

In Florida, for instance, a 1990 survey found that 28 percent of teachers reported that they had "refrained from teaching a controversial topic or book in the classroom for fear of complaints or retribution." In 1986 when a textbook containing two classics— *Lysistrata*, by Aristophanes, and Chaucer's *The Miller's Tale*—was removed from classrooms in Columbia County, school officials in nearby Putnam County also dropped the book and ordered a new text, although they had not received any complaints about the old one.[38]

The 1980 AAP-ALA-ASCD survey found that, in nearly 85 percent of the reported challenges, there was no media coverage; and in only a fourth of the incidents did school or community groups become involved—either in support or in opposition. This lack of broad community involvement may well deprive schools of a potential safeguard against censorship from within by administrators or staff members who may not necessarily reflect the views of the entire community. Indeed, one school superintendent revealed that a censorial mentality underpinned his district's selection procedures: "With all the good literature available, it would be my hope we could accentuate the best and leave a lot of the questionable stuff off the shelves and the reading lists," this administrator wrote. "Wish the publishers could do a better job of sorting originally."

Still other comments suggested that some censorship results from the "chilling effect" of previous controversy and the desire to avoid conflict. One principal reported, "Parental badgering has caused rifts between teachers and administrators. Extreme care is taken in selecting any material." Another superintendent wrote simply, "We really try not to select controversial materials going in."[39]

In the Denver area, where challenges to instructional and library materials were frequent in the mid-1980s, teachers openly acknowledged that the pressures had a chilling effect, even though not a single challenge was successful. "I've consciously made the decision, 'No, this is risky,' and I don't use the material I think will produce phone calls," explained one English teacher. "If I were challenged, I think I'd win, but I can't waste my resources. Meeting after meeting and ugly phone calls and threatening rumors really are draining and take away from what I'm supposed to be accomplishing."

"Though you may say one thing in public, it's easy to make those subtle changes that do impoverish what you're teaching without ever owning up to it," a social studies teacher said. "The most powerful and important changes will happen inside the classrooms without teachers saying anything about it."[40]

If they are to work, policies and procedures must be followed. In preparing its 1990–91 report, *Attacks on the Freedom to Learn*, People for the American Way determined that in incidents where review processes were in place and followed, 74 percent resulted in retention of the challenged materials. Where policies were not followed, or where there was no policy, only 46 percent resulted in retention.[41] In her extensive survey study, Professor Hopkins found that although most respondents had a board-approved materials selection policy, use of the policy during the challenge process varied considerably, with 37 percent of responses indicating the policy was not used at all, and only 25 percent confirming that its provisions were fully followed.[42]

According to the ACLU survey of four southern states, school librarians in Alabama, Louisiana, and Tennessee reported that policy was completely followed in less than a third of the challenges filed. Only in Georgia was policy followed more often than not—and then, just barely, at a reported level of 50.5 percent. One Georgia librarian reported that "the policy is rarely followed. Usually if there is a challenge, the book is removed from the shelf by the school principal." From Tennessee, a respondent wrote: "Books questioned are immediately removed from circulation . . . Anything found with four-letter words is usually questioned. Principal demands removal from shelf. Librarian is given no voice in the matter." An Alabama librarian reported that the "people 'in charge' are censors themselves."

It should be stressed that school administrators who ignore established policies and procedures in removing a book—or districts that have no policy and therefore can be said to have acted arbitrarily—probably place themselves in legal jeopardy. But, even more important, responses such as these point to the existence of widespread self-censorship, which may amount to as great a danger to education as any external censorship pressures.

A Louisiana librarian wrote, "My main observation is that teachers, librarians, media personnel, and supervisors practice self-censorship—'Let's do it for them before they do it to us,' seems to be the prevailing attitude. Most of the time, the people doing the censoring do it out of fear [and] misinformation and they usually are very professional otherwise." Volunteered a Tennessee librarian: "I have concluded that most censorship occurs by the librarians themselves. They avoid buying materials that may be deemed questionable."[43]

One important purpose of this book is to make available to school administrators, teachers, and librarians knowledge and skills essential for dealing with censorship pressures and for planning the selection of instructional and library materials. Central to these tasks is the formulation of policies and procedures that defend intellectual freedom, while simultaneously guaranteeing the individual complainant's right to be heard. But the most eloquent statements in support of academic freedom, the most carefully crafted policies, and the fairest procedures will be useless if these are not founded upon a more fundamental commitment to diversity and free expression.

Misguided censorship efforts aimed at instructional and school library materials can be readily defeated. Would-be censors are often very effective at making a great deal of noise. More often than not, however, all the sound and fury truly signify nothing. Censors need education; they need to be educated in the ways of democracy. But educators, too, need educating. Without a full understanding of the problem and of how to deal with it they may fight the wrong battle or sink into the mire of self-censorship.

2

Arenas of Conflict

Libraries should provide materials and information presenting all points of view on current and historical issues. Materials should not be proscribed or removed because of partisan or doctrinal disapproval.

American Library Association,
Library Bill of Rights[1]

Some people think that if we study something in a book, that condones it. There is no reason to think because something is portrayed in a book that the school is sanctioning that attitude.

June Berkley, Department of English,
Ohio University[2]

I'm not even sure any more where children's rights begin and parental rights leave off. I'm not sure that children don't have the right to read what they want to read even if their parents object to it.

author Judy Blume[3]

School censorship controversies may differ according to what kind of material is challenged and how that material is used in the school. School libraries have been the principal targets of efforts to remove or restrict materials, even though, in general, students are not compelled to make use of library resources. Although school libraries differ from public libraries in their mission and in the community they serve, as libraries they remain repositories of information, opinion, and representations, where all sides of every issue should be available.

Materials used in the classroom, including textbooks, supplementary readings, and audio-visual aids, differ from library materials insofar as students are generally required to use them. Whereas the library's role is to allow the student to explore vast realms of knowledge and ideas, classroom instruction strives principally to develop specified skills and to convey essential information. Although would-be censors frequently fail to distinguish between the school library and the classroom, these are two very different arenas of conflict. Principles of intellectual and academic freedom apply to both, but in somewhat different ways.

As already noted, academic freedom includes the right of students to question, to learn, and to express themselves. The students' right to learn has increasingly been understood to embrace a right to express controversial ideas, in written assignments, informally in class discussion, and, in many schools, in publications of their own. The student press and other media of student expression have emerged as yet a third arena where censorship conflict may occur.

The School Library and the Library Bill of Rights

Librarians have long been in the forefront of opposition to censorship. This should not be surprising, since libraries—as repositories of information, images, and ideas—must be free to acquire and provide materials without prejudice or restriction. It is in the library that students are free to learn to the limits of their abilities and to the limits of what is known. Courts have acknowledged the central importance of libraries in a system that cherishes freedom of expression.

The American Library Association and the library profession have developed principles, institutions, and programs that promote intellectual freedom and oppose censorship. The Library Bill of Rights, which derives from a statement originally developed by the Des Moines Public Library nearly 50 years ago, is ALA's basic policy on intellectual freedom and librarianship. Along with its several "interpretations," this document provides an unambiguous statement in support of the library's role as guardian of diverse opinion and a resource for all. It is intended to apply to school libraries as well as public and research libraries, and should be directly incorporated in every school library selection policy. (The complete text of the Library Bill of Rights follows. Three of its interpretations are included in Appendixes A, B, and C.)

According to the ALA document, "Access to Resources and Services in the School Library Media Program," first adopted in 1986 and amended in 1990 (see appendix A):

> The school library media program plays a unique role in promoting intellectual freedom. It serves as a point of voluntary access to information and ideas and as a learning laboratory for students as they acquire critical thinking and problem solving skills needed in a pluralistic society. Although the educational level and program of the school necessarily shapes the resources and services of a school library media program, the principles of the Library Bill of Rights apply equally to all libraries, including school library media programs.[4]

The Library Bill of Rights commits each and every library to providing information and enlightenment to all people in the community served by the library, regardless of origin, background, views, or age. "Free Access to Libraries for Minors: An Interpretation of the Library

Library Bill of Rights

The American Library Association affirms that all libraries are forums for information and ideas, and that the following basic policies should guide their services. Adopted June 18, 1948. Amended February 2, 1961, and January 23, 1980, by the ALA Council.

1. Books and other library resources should be provided for the interest, information, and enlightenment of all people of the community the library serves. Materials should not be excluded because of the origin, background, or views of those contributing to their creation.
2. Libraries should provide materials and information presenting all points of view on current and historical issues. Materials should not be proscribed or removed because of partisan or doctrinal disapproval.
3. Libraries should challenge censorship in the fulfillment of their responsibility to provide information and enlightenment.
4. Libraries should cooperate with all persons and groups concerned with resisting abridgment of free expression and free access to ideas.
5. A person's right to use a library should not be denied or abridged because of origin, age, background, or views.
6. Libraries which make exhibit spaces and meeting rooms available to the public they serve should make such facilities available on an equitable basis, regardless of the beliefs or affiliations of individuals or groups requesting their use.

Bill of Rights" (see appendix B) notes further: "Librarians have a professional commitment to ensure that all members of the community they serve have free and equal access to the entire range of library resources regardless of content, approach, format, or amount of detail. This principle of library service applies equally to all users, minors as well as adults." This document also emphasizes "that parents—and only parents—have the right and the responsibility to restrict the access of their children—and only their children—to library resources. Parents or legal guardians who do not want their children to have access to certain library services, materials or facilities, should so advise their children."[5]

Of course, the school library serves a community composed entirely (or nearly entirely) of minors, and this necessarily influences selection policies. Nevertheless, the American Library Association holds that building library collections to fit the needs of school library users need not limit young readers' access to controversial materials. The appropriateness of a book for a school library should be determined principally on the basis of its relevance to the overall school curriculum and by the reading level to which it is directed, and not according to potential controversy surrounding its content. To take an admittedly extreme example: An elementary school library will avoid purchasing works of advanced political and social theory or adult literature—not because these should be denied to some precocious pupil willing to give them a try, but only because such precocity is quite rare, and purchase of such materials would be an obvious waste of limited resources.

The relatively narrow age spectrum of the school library's clientele can become an excuse for censorship. Materials might be removed from elementary or junior high school libraries and reshelved at a higher level because they are allegedly inappropriate for the younger grades. In fact, they simply may not meet some censor's standard. In Peoria, Illinois, in 1984, three books by Judy Blume, *Then Again, Maybe I Won't, Deenie*, and *Blubber*, were restricted to older students. The action amounted to a kind of censorship, since the lead character in *Deenie* is a seventh grader and *Blubber* was written for fifth-grade readers. By placing these books in a high school library, school officials guaranteed they would not be read.[6]

Other means of imposing effective censorship on school library patrons include requiring permissions from parents or teachers; establishing restricted shelves or closed collections; and labeling or expurgating works. These activities violate the Library Bill of Rights.

The School Library: Selection Policies

Selection policies need to accommodate quite varied levels of intellectual development among students, as well as diverse family backgrounds and child-rearing philosophies of parents. As "Free Access to Libraries for Minors" notes: "Librarians cannot predict what resources will best fulfill the needs and interests of any individual user based on a single criterion such as chronological age, level of education, or legal emancipation."[7] The period of time during which children are interested in reading materials specifically designed for them grows steadily shorter, and librarians must recognize and adjust to this change if they wish to serve young people effectively.

The Library Bill of Rights mandates inclusion of "materials and information presenting all points of view." As elaborated in the ALA document, "Diversity in Collection Development" (see appendix C), this means:

> Librarians have a professional responsibility to be inclusive, not exclusive. . . . Access to all materials legally obtainable should be assured to the user and policies should not unjustly exclude materials even if offensive to the librarian or the user. . . . A balanced collection reflects a diversity of materials, not an equality of numbers. . . . Collection development and the selection of materials should be done according to professional standards and established selection and review procedures. . . . Librarians have an obligation to protect library collections from removal of materials based on personal bias or prejudice, and to select and support the access to materials on all subjects that meet, as closely as possible, the needs and interests of all persons in the community which the library serves. This includes materials that reflect political, economic, religious, social, minority, and sexual issues.[8]

Few educators and not many others would challenge the central importance of these principles for university and research libraries and for the overwhelming majority of public libraries, although public library censorship is also a significant problem. But strict application of the Library Bill of Rights to school libraries troubles many. The public library, some argue, is a community resource open to all to use as they see fit. By contrast, the school library is part of a larger educational structure whose goal is to mold young minds. The situation of the school library is also complicated because the librarian shares responsibility with the teachers, and both are responsible to higher authorities—the school principal, district administrators and, ultimately, the board of education.

As one federal judge put it in a discussion of the censorship issue:

Suppose they went out and bought a book teaching genocide. Suppose—I mean, just this principle that every idea is fine and can be in a library. Suppose they glorified Hitler or preached mass murder of Jews. Or take an example in a high school, suppose they had in a library a book which white children were taking out that was preaching inherent inferiority of blacks and it was disrupting things in the school. You have to have some limit on what you want kids to read. Don't you really? I mean, do you really want them to read a book preaching genocide?[9]

Let us look for a moment at one book that does, in essence, preach genocide—Adolf Hitler's *Mein Kampf*. Few, if any, educators would recommend this book to a student seeking to formulate an individual political perspective. But can a high school library adequately fulfill its mission in a school where a history course covering the Nazi experience is taught, if the fundamental document of the Nazi movement cannot be found for student reference? In such a situation, *Mein Kampf*—along with other more objective treatments of Hitler's thought—would probably be in the high school library, funding and space permitting.

But, it may be objected, a book that is purchased and shelved for reference purposes, to help students write term papers and learn to analyze controversial materials, will not necessarily be used solely in this manner. What if a little "Hitler cult" emerges in the school and students begin to read *Mein Kampf*—or some more contemporary racist work—not as an historical or political document, but as a meaningful tract for our times?

The situation is troubling, but censorship offers no solution. If there is a problem with racism in a school, removing materials from the library will not solve it. Indeed, like other efforts to drive the problem underground, such removals may only exacerbate matters. A good school librarian will work with teachers and school officials continually to take the pulse of student interests. If a segment of the student body seems inordinately attracted to materials that run counter to the purposes of democratic education, then the faculty and staff must work to expose the weaknesses of these materials by discussing them with the students—in class if need be—and by directing students to positive alternatives.

One special role played by the school library is to educate students about what libraries are. Students should be taught at an early age that the presence of a book in a library, including in the school library, does not mean that the book is somehow "endorsed" by the librarian or the school. The library is a resource that caters to varied interests; it is *a place to go to find out for oneself*. This lesson cannot be taught, however, if the school library is not such a place, if the student is in effect told: Come here to find out the things you want to know, but only if established authorities approve them in advance. The school library has an important role to play in educating young people to respect diversity by itself illustrating the breadth of diverse opinion and taste.

The Classroom

Although school libraries seem most vulnerable to censorship pressures, recent reports suggest that challenges are increasingly focused on classroom instructional materials, including textbooks. Instructional materials used in class differ from library materials insofar as students are generally compelled to use specified works in class, whereas in the library they are given a choice. In theory, a library can be expanded to include all approaches to a given subject area, to accommodate almost every taste. But in a course of study a single textbook is often used, sometimes along with a limited number of supplementary materials. Certainly, charges that efforts to remove instructional materials amount to unwarranted censorship are more difficult to sustain than in the corresponding case of the library since, in the classroom, the key element of choice, if not entirely lacking, is surely restricted.

Textbooks must be selected carefully both for accuracy and for sensitivity to community and minority feelings. This is one reason why, in many states, textbooks may be selected only from a list approved by state education authorities. In California, a series of social studies texts published by Houghton Mifflin came under fire in a series of heated meetings before the state Board of Education. Many different religious, ethnic, and racial groups unsuccessfully criticized the books for a lack of cultural diversity and alleged Eurocentrism. The books were commissioned by state education officials as part of a new multicultural curriculum and supporters contend the books, while not perfect, are a vast improvement over previous social studies materials. Although school districts were not compelled to purchase the texts, without a special waiver the state would not approve the full cost of alternate materials. Nevertheless, the financially strapped Oakland Board of Education voted against the books, compelling teachers to rely on xeroxed materials and other makeshift teaching aids.[10]

Since 1987 dozens of school districts in all parts of the country have encountered controversy over a series of elementary school reading texts published by Harcourt Brace Jovanovich under the overall title *Impressions*. Although sometimes used as required textbooks, the teachers are frequently challenged even when districts use them only on a supplementary basis.

Initially, those who objected to the books charged that they were too morbid and displayed disrespect for parents and authority in general. As the controversy entered the legal arena, however, opponents of *Impressions* began to assert that use of the books is unconstitutional, since they violate the separation of church and state by promoting "the religions of witchcraft and neopaganism," to use the language of one lawsuit. On April 2, 1992, however, United States District Court in Sacramento, California, ruled that "there is no constitutional basis for the court to order that the activities in question be excluded from the classroom simply because isolated instances of those activities may happen to coincide or harmonize with the tenets of two relatively obscure religions."[11] Two similar decisions were handed down by courts in Illinois.

Increasingly controversy at the local level also has arisen around supplementary classroom materials. Novels and plays read for discussion in English class or chosen by an individual student from a "recommended" list for a book report have become targets of criticism despite the fact that in most instances students were offered several alternatives. In countless such incidents irate parents or others have sought the removal of such books from all classroom activities, required or optional.

While many would-be censors do not care to draw very fine distinctions, others have been careful to note that, while they would not mind the presence of a given book in the school library, they do object to its assignment in class or to its presence on a recommended reading list that would seem to imply school endorsement of its content. In Virginia, a parent who challenged John Steinbeck's *Of Mice and Men*, stressed "that a book like this should not be required reading. If they want to have it in the library that's fine, but it shouldn't be required." In that case, the school declined to remove the book from the curriculum, but agreed to provide substitute assignments for any offended families.[12]

In a Florida case that wound up in court, however, a school board ordered the removal to locked storage of a literature textbook containing excerpts from the classic Greek comedy *Lysistrata*, by Aristophanes and *The Miller's Tale*, by the medieval English poet Geoffrey Chaucer, because of parental complaints of "explicit sexuality and excessively vulgar language." Although a federal appeals court felt compelled to "seriously question how young persons just below the age of majority can be harmed by these masterpieces of Western literature," the board's action was upheld. The court focused on the fact that these were materials used within the curriculum and thus could be understood to bear the imprimatur of school approval. It then found that the reason for the removal—sexuality and vulgar language—was a legitimate pedagogical concern. The court also found the board action reasonable because the textbook, as well as other versions of the disputed selections, remained available in the school library.[13]

Also targeted have been movies, videotapes, and filmstrips; guest speakers; newspaper and magazine articles; student dramatic productions; and various classroom exercises suggested in teacher manuals or other sources. Sometimes whole curriculum modules have proved controversial. Not surprisingly, these often involve sex education, like the Michigan Model for Comprehensive School Health Education. Increasingly, however, counseling and "self-esteem" units like the "DUSO," "Pumsy" and Quest programs have been targeted for removal from schools because, it is alleged, they undercut "family values" or parental authority. In several South Carolina counties the "Pumsy in Pursuit of Excellence" program, in which a dragon puppet is used to encourage self-esteem and critical thinking skills among elementary school pupils, has been challenged as an unwarranted religious intrusion in public education. Opponents of the program charge that it incorporates Eastern mysticism and New Age philosophy.[14]

Again, what must be stressed is that simply reading and studying a book or other work of expression does not necessarily imply full endorsement of its contents—especially with respect to literature, but also with reference to political and some scientific works. Teachers must be free to present students with alternatives and choices if students are to be trained to make intelligent and informed decisions on their own. This is a fundamental principle of education. Unfortunately, many parents and citizens do not fully comprehend this principle, and so schools must endeavor to explain it.

In some instances, nonetheless, parents may still firmly believe that any exposure to certain materials will somehow prove "damaging" to their child. The Supreme Court has given some support to parents who take this position on the basis of religious convictions. In a 1972 case, Amish parents won the right to remove their children from school and instead teach them at home because of a conflict between their religious values and the lessons emphasized in the public school attended by the children. However, parental objections that are based on personal or philosophical grounds, rather than religious reasons, do not enjoy Constitutional protection.[15] Moreover, the courts generally have not supported efforts by objecting parents to *change* the curriculum or otherwise impose their beliefs on the schools.

Where possible, schools should respect parental beliefs, insofar as the parents do not attempt to impose them on others. Where it is not disruptive, there is nothing wrong with assigning an alternate reading for a student whose family finds a given work offensive, especially in the case of required book reports or other "outside reading" assignments. Such a policy can only go so far, though. In the final analysis, it is the responsibility of the educator and not the parent to determine the curriculum. No public school system could survive if it were compelled to tailor whole courses of study to individual family demands. Once a textbook is selected for a course, it should be used by all. Assignment of an occasional alternate reading indicates flexibility, not the abdication of authority.

In one widely publicized 1987 case, several fundamentalist families in Church Hill, Tennessee, challenged an elementary school reading program for using books and materials that they described as "anti-Christian." The parents asked that their children be dismissed from class when the offending reading texts were used and that they be provided with alternate materials. Although initially the Hawkins County school system tried to accommodate them, officials found that this placed too much strain on the system. The parents won the initial round in their challenge, but the United States Court of Appeals reversed a prior court order that would have institutionalized the system of dismissing the children from reading assignments that parents found objectionable. The appellate court reasoned that the First Amendment did not require the school system to cater to the parents' religious beliefs, and that the parents had failed to prove that the act of reading amounted to a governmental compulsion to adopt the views expressed in the required texts.[16]

The Student Press

In 1969, the United States Supreme Court first explicitly recognized that public school students enjoy First Amendment rights. In *Tinker v. Des Moines Independent Community School District*, the Court issued its now-famous ruling that neither "students [n]or teachers shed their rights to freedom of speech or expression at the schoolhouse gate."[17]

The *Tinker* case concerned the right of students to wear armbands of protest against the Vietnam War in school. But the ramifications of the high court's decision have been widespread. Other federal and state courts have applied the principles enumerated in *Tinker* to diverse forms of student expression, including speech and student journalism. Considerable controversy has arisen, especially over the rights of the student press—both officially sponsored curricular and extracurricular newspapers, journals, and yearbooks; and so-called "underground" publications.

Court decisions treating the rights and responsibilities of student journalists have varied (see chapter 6). In January 1988, the Supreme Court decided its first student press case, *Hazelwood School District v. Kuhlmeier.* In that case, a principal removed two pages of a newspaper produced by a high school journalism class containing articles on teenage pregnancy and the impact of divorce on students. The principal defended his action on the grounds that he was protecting the privacy of the pregnant students described, protecting younger students from inappropriate references to sexual activity and birth control, and protecting the school from a potential libel action.

The decision contrasted dramatically with previous rulings by federal and state courts across the country handed down over the previous fifteen years that had given student journalists extensive First Amendment protections. Reversing an appellate court decision that had favored student journalists, the Court ruled that the First Amendment is not violated when an educator exercises "editorial control over the style and content of student speech" that is part of a "curricular" activity if that speech is inconsistent with the school's basic educational mission. "It is only when the decision to censor a school-sponsored publication, theatrical production, or other vehicle of student expression has no valid educational purpose that the First Amendment is so 'directly and sharply implicate[d],' as to require judicial intervention to protect students' constitutional rights," the Court declared.[18]

The *Hazelwood* decision lent support to the concern of some school administrators that the unfettering of inexperienced and immature student journalists can affect the climate of a school and pose virtually insoluble disciplinary problems. But if the decision granted school administrators greater authority over content, like all court decisions upholding government authority to restrict expression, it by no means mandated or even recommended greater exercise of that authority. Whatever restrictions may now legally be placed on some school journalists, the question of student press regulation remains inextricably entwined with broader issues of censorship and academic freedom. Efforts by teachers and school officials to influence the content of student publications may open another door to censorship of educational materials more generally. Pressures exerted on student journalists, if successful, may encourage additional pressures on teachers and librarians to remove or restrict access to instructional and library materials.

Although administrators' fears about discipline and disruption may not lightly be dismissed, the more central matter of concern is the role of student publications in the educational process. The student press offers one important means of keeping students informed about the world in which they live. Students who find it difficult to understand or trust adult publications may place a higher value on information conveyed in their own idiom by journalists who are their peers. Young people may be woefully uninformed about the most important issues that directly affect their lives, including such potentially controversial matters as birth control, abortion, drug abuse, and even school funding and administration. Most professional journalists and educators believe that the student press should be free, within boundaries clearly established by the appropriate school authorities, to address responsibly these types of issues, regardless of pressures exerted by varied elements within the schools or the community.

Perhaps even more important, like the school library, student journalism offers young people initial experience with an institution they will encounter and use for their entire lives. Their crucial initial understanding of the role and functioning of these institutions will be established in the school.

Unfortunately, what is a student to believe when taught about a free press and the First Amendment in class if the free expression of the school's own journalists is suppressed? As *New York Times* columnist Tom Wicker put it: "All too many of these high school editors and reporters may well conclude, from hard experience, that freedom of the press is as bad a joke as the ones school boards would like for them to print in place of news and opinion; and holding that cynical view they are far more likely to become doctors, engineers, or politicians than reporters. If they do become reporters, having felt the knife so early, they are not likely to stick their necks out in the name of the First Amendment."[19]

Certainly, the student press plays a role in the closed society of a school not unlike the role its commercial counterpart plays in society at large. Its mission should be to provide a forum for members of the school community to voice opinions about issues of concern, and to do so free of outside censorship.

3

Issues in Dispute

Democracy is dependent upon the right of people to study and discuss issues freely, ... it is dependent upon the citizenry ... which keeps well informed, searches actively for divergent points of view, evaluates courses of action in the light of available evidence and basic democratic values. ... Such behaviors do not develop by accident; they are learned in the schools within the context of societal problems, many of which are controversial in nature.

National Association of Secondary School Principals[1]

There are almost as many motivations to censor as there are would-be censors. A school curriculum or library that does not arouse the ire of someone in our pluralistic society is probably not fully succeeding in its educational mission.

To be sure, some objections that have been lodged against educational materials are just silly. Others are based on a readily corrected misjudgment of the material. In one now famous instance, for example, a challenge was filed against a library book called *Making It with Mademoiselle*, which turned out to be a volume of sewing patterns. In one Florida county *Snow White*—the traditional Grimm Brothers telling, not the Disney version—cannot be checked out in elementary schools without parental permission because of its violence. Elsewhere in Florida *Little Red Riding Hood* was pulled from schools after teachers questioned a passage in which the young girl takes her grandmother wine.[2] In the majority of cases, however, controversy emerges when a complaint is seriously and sincerely supported by a significant body of opinion in the community.

Recent efforts to remove or restrict access to school library or instructional materials have been most associated with politically conservative or fundamentalist religious views. However, those who object to materials come from all points on the ideological spectrum. Liberal activists fighting against race and gender stereotyping have sometimes used censorious tactics they are quick to condemn in others. Many conservatives are also staunch opponents of censorship, and religious leaders frequently have proved valuable allies for besieged educators fighting censorship attempts.

As a rule, the motives and concerns of complainants cannot be easily pigeon-holed into neatly labeled boxes. The political and social climate varies widely from community to community and over time. What is controversial today becomes orthodoxy tomorrow, and vice versa. It is, however, still possible to identify several key issues and concerns around which recent censorship controversies have tended to cluster.

Politics

It is, perhaps, a credit to our democracy that relatively few challenges are lodged for blatantly political reasons. Although occasionally a work is charged with promoting "Communism" or "Marxism," or even simply the Democrats or the Republicans, more often than not the underlying concerns motivating such charges are moral. The notion that students should learn about diverse political philosophies and creeds, including those hostile to commonly accepted American principles, seems fairly well accepted.

Still, complaints have been lodged by some self-described conservatives against certain history and social studies texts for an alleged bias against the free enterprise system, or even the Republican Party. In some such cases extreme charges have been made against textbooks issued by responsible, mainstream publishers and judged by teachers —liberal and conservative, Democrat and Republican—to be generally accurate and moderate.

In San Bernardino, California, a series of eleven educational films on ethnic issues in American history was rejected by a school board in part because the portrayal of Castro's Cuba in one film allegedly contained "un-American propaganda," although one board member complained more about "the use of four-letter words."[3] In Alabama, the state textbook committee rejected a text entitled *Americans All*, which came under political fire from both conservatives and feminists.

The latter complained that the book used the word suffragette rather than suffragist to describe those who fought for women's right to vote. Conservative critics charged the book with lavishing "praise on blacks, women, labor unions, and Democrats," while criticizing "just about everything that Americans have accomplished."[4]

Objections have also come from the other end of the political spectrum. In recent years there has been much talk about attempts to impose a left-liberal agenda of so-called "political correctness" in many colleges and universities. The issue has not much been raised with reference to elementary and secondary education. In Amherst, Massachusetts, however, a group of liberal parents complained that an eighth-grade social studies text oversimplified events and presented them in a conservative light. They said *The History of the American Nation* was "unforgivably misleading and biased" in its presentation of minority groups, women, the Civil Rights movement, and the Vietnam War. Even the book's title posed a problem. Said one parent: "It's an implicit denial of the existence of other American nations, such as Canada and Mexico and the countries of Central and South America."[5]

Since the first edition of this book was published, political controversies over environmental protection have begun to produce censorship pressures. In Pennsylvania, one school board rejected an Environmental Science text as "extremely biased" and too "politically correct" and another turned down a gift to school libraries of two animal-rights books. In Oregon, where logging interests and environmentalists have clashed, objections were raised to a library book, *Eli's Songs*, which was labeled "logger bashing" and "a political book geared to children" by petitioners in a rural school district. "We are gravely concerned regarding the 'eco-mania' that is being pushed on our children in the classroom," the petitioners declared. In the most publicized such incident, in 1989 a rural northern California school board defeated an attempt to remove *The Lorax*, by Dr. Seuss, from its second grade core reading list because of the book's alleged hostility to the timber industry.[6]

Sometimes objections raised on moral, social, or religious grounds may be joined to or reflect prejudices shaped by political ideology. For instance, in one Wisconsin school district the Vietnam War film *Hearts and Minds* was banned by the superintendent after teachers refused to excise a brothel scene. The teachers decided that, rather than show a censored version, they wouldn't show the film at all. Apparently, some people on both sides of the dispute found it difficult to separate the film's alleged sexual content from its antiwar political stance. Although the order to edit the film violated district policy at the time, the school

board voted to uphold the decision. Several months later the board
again overruled a reconsideration committee vote to permit screenings
of the film.[7]

"Global Education"

One unusual, but illuminating, example of an effort to remove materials for explicitly political reasons occurred in Colorado in 1985, where
strong opposition was voiced to materials from a program in "global
education" offered by the University of Denver's Center for Teaching
International Relations.[8] Although the protests espoused nationalistic
and isolationist views, the rejection of "globalism" could also be interpreted as a fearful and defensive response to cultural and political
diversity.

The campaign against "global education" originated with a report
written by two Denver-based federal education officials. They labeled
the global education program a "left-wing monopoly" and charged that
its materials for schools were "pacifistic," "capitulationist," and "biased
toward radical political change." Global education, they alleged, "attacks the institutions that are the cornerstone of our society" in a quest
for a pro-Soviet one-world government. Although the Education Department did not approve the report, some parents reacted to its
charges with alarm. In Longmont, Colorado, a concerned grandparent,
who said he'd read the report, objected to a booklet produced by the
Denver Center which stated that children should strive to set aside
ethnocentric attitudes. "I definitely think my nation is superior to all
others," he said, "and I'll be damned if I'll set aside my ethnocentric
attitudes." In rural Bennett, a third of the district's 65 teachers left the
district as a result of the protests.

Most of the furor focused on fewer than a dozen booklets in a series
of about 75 supplemental activity handbooks produced by the Center,
which were used by 10 Colorado districts. In 1985, the Center also
trained about 1,000 teachers in use of the materials and in "global
education" precepts. The booklets were designed for use by teachers
and not as textbooks for students. In many instances, the material
found objectionable was actually presented as one of several alternative viewpoints.

Although the controversy in Colorado was admittedly an extreme
case, concern about "one-worldism" has motivated other censorship
efforts. In Alabama, two members of a conservative women's group,

charged that a state-approved history book, *World History for a Global Age*, sanctions "one-worldism," instills fear of nuclear war, and "promotes the idea that the United States is an imperialistic nation whereas Russia is not."[9]

"Dirty" Words

A frequent objection, especially against library books, is that they use "inappropriate" language or are even "obscene" or "pornographic." Almost half the districts reporting challenges to the 1987 AASA survey conducted for the first edition of this book indicated complaints had been filed against materials with "dirty" words. In 1992, an Oregon school board limited access to a reference thesaurus because of the presence of racial epithets and slang words for sex and drugs.[10] Often, the issue of language is closely entwined with that of "moral values." A work may be challenged because it does not promote, or is even hostile to, the traditional family and traditional moral principles. The evidence offered to support this charge may be limited to the presence of one or more "four-letter words."

In one Florida community the school board banned from a middle school library an oral history of the Vietnam War that used harsh language. Commenting on *Bloods: An Oral History of the Vietnam War by Black Veterans*, compiled by Wallace Terry, the school board attorney said foul language was unnecessary. "I served in a war myself," he said, "and I don't feel I need to revert to that language to recall my experiences." But others disagreed, arguing that the soldiers' harsh language was consistent with their experiences. "You wouldn't expect them to say 'Gloriosky!'" one parent remarked.

The school media specialist filed a grievance, charging that the book was removed without an opinion from the school's Media Center Advisory Committee, as required by district policy. The school board upheld the principal, arguing that the presence of objectionable language in a book "is a matter of imminent danger to the students." In this case the board received some questionable advice from its attorney, who said, "You cannot allow segments of society to control your library" by claiming First Amendment rights, which, he charged, are often "prostituted."

In fact, as the courts have frequently recognized, removal of materials poses a far greater threat to education than demands by those exercising First Amendment rights for the inclusion of materials. An ACLU attorney correctly informed the board that a school principal, no less than other complainants, must follow the board's review process. To avoid situations where "an individual's values are allowed to be so dominant," the ACLU recommended that "the principal put *all* complaints—no matter where they originate—through the review committee."[11]

A complaint about language was more effectively handled in Stoughton, Wisconsin, where an effort to remove Harry Mazer's novel, *Snow Bound*, from a middle school reading program was resolved to everyone's satisfaction. The district's review committee suggested that parents be notified when the book is assigned and offered an alternative assignment where appropriate. The parent had originally asked that the book be "withdrawn from all students" because of several profane oaths, two four-letter words for bodily wastes, and use of the terms "crazy bitch" and "stupid female" by a character.[12]

Profanity and Policy

A policy of parental notification should be adopted only with great caution, however. With respect to library materials, such a policy is generally not advisable, both for reasons of principle and practicality. Assigned classroom reading is admittedly a more complex issue, because the student is not usually free to choose assignments. Still, teachers who are compelled to always inform parents about the use of language *someone* might find objectionable will not only be burdened with unnecessary paperwork but, more important, may tend to select assigned readings according to the standards of the most restrictive families, thus trampling on the rights of the others.

In Alamo Heights, Texas, almost two hundred parents petitioned the school board "to add a selection criterion that instructional resource material shall not contain vulgar or profane language." Such a blanket rule is not recommended, however. More appropriate is the policy of the Lincoln, Nebraska, schools, which states explicitly that materials containing profanity "shall not be disqualified automatically, but shall be subjected to a test of merit and suitability."[13] It is true, of course, that, "Freedom of speech was not intended to guarantee schools the right to intrude on traditional family values without warning and regardless of the availability of nonoffensive alternatives," as one Lincoln parent protesting the use of the words "lord," "damn," "snotty," and "shut up" in the Newbery Award-winning novel *Bridge to Tarabithia* declared. But parents who are especially concerned about their children's contact with this sort of language must themselves take responsibility to more carefully monitor their children's reading. The schools cannot and should not do this for them.

"Great care must be used not to abandon quality works of literature that may offend individual patrons," the Lincoln school board concluded in the *Tarabithia* case. The fear that quality will suffer is not unfounded. In Kentucky, a parent labeled Nobel Prize winner William Faulkner's *As I Lay Dying* "pure filth" after "browsing through" its pages and finding profanity. "I believe I have an open mind and I can accept some cussing. But not like this," she said. The book was removed from classrooms, although it was returned a week later after embarrassing national publicity. In Maryland, another parent objected to the language in the Faulkner novel and in Henrik Ibsen's play, *Ghosts. The Grapes of Wrath* and *Of Mice and Men*, by John Steinbeck, another Nobel Prize winner, are favored targets of censors for their use of so-called "dirty" words. In 1992 over a thousand people in Tennessee signed a petition against *Of Mice and Men*, protesting its "blasphemous" language. In Ohio, one parent charged that the book contains 108 profanities, 12 racial slurs, and uses God's name in vain 45 times.[14]

In Mount Vernon, Washington, a parent who objected to use of "the F-word" in a novel her daughter found in her middle school library declared, "It's hypocritical for the school to prohibit obscenity but to provide it in the school library." A similar sentiment was voiced in Lamar, Missouri, birthplace of Harry Truman, where J.D. Salinger's *The Catcher in the Rye*, a favorite censor's target, was dropped from an optional reading list after a school board member objected to its use of obscenities. "If a child talks that way during class," he said, "they will be suspended. Why should it be okay to read and teach the same things?"[15]

The answer, of course, is, first of all, that students whose classroom language is inappropriate, rarely, if ever, have learned to speak this way from literature. "If you could look on the [school] bus, this would be a *Little Bo Beep* story," quipped one eleven-year-old in defense of *The Chocolate War*, by Robert Cormier, a popular novel attacked in Connecticut (and many other places) for its language.[16] Contemporary students are able to distinguish between discussions *about* language and the indiscriminate use of certain words. They can understand that literature and life are not identical; that the representation of reality through fiction is not the same as reality itself. It must be stressed that when characters in fiction use obscenity or profanity, this does not mean the author *advocates* the use of such language. (See "Why 'Dirty Words' in Books?") Unfortunately, this is not always clear to those who protest.

Why "Dirty Words" in Books?
An Author Explains

In a 1979 letter to a young reader, author Robin Brancato, a former high school English teacher, explained why she uses "bad language" in her popular novels for young adult readers. She wrote:

I suppose I don't like "bad language" any more than you do. The main trouble with it from my point of view is that it is boring, unimaginative, and lazy. In conversation it often fills in where original and interesting language ought to be. However, my business as a writer is not so much to pass judgment on how people speak, but to try to record their speech accurately for the sake of telling a story whose underlying values, I hope, are moral and positive.

When I employ "bad language," as you call it, and references to sex, it is not because I think these are needed to sell books or to hold the reader's interest, but because sex and body functions and the names for them, both polite and impolite, are parts of life, and I am interested in portraying life as it really is. If I fudge on details by creating an angry football player who says, "Oh, sugar!", who will trust me later, when I try to convey the important things that athletes think and feel?

I could, of course, choose to write only about people who use good language, but that would eliminate a lot of possibilities for characters. I guess what it comes down to is that even though I, too, dislike bad language, that doesn't keep me from liking or even loving a lot of people who use it. I want them in my books, too, even at the risk of offending a few readers.

I hope that you will continue your interest in reading and language. I hope that fewer people in the future will feel the need to use lazy, unimaginative language, so that it will fade away and I won't have to put it in my books. And I also hope that you will come to agree with me that what is more important in judging people in both real life and literature is not the purity of their language but the goodness of their spirits.

Reprinted from Norma Klein. "Some Thoughts on Censorship: An Author Symposium." *Top of the News,* Winter 1983, p. 139.

In one California elementary school, the novel *Anastasia Krupnik*, by Lois Lowry, was simply returned by school authorities to the library with two offensive four-letter words whited out.[17] Such practices violate democratic principles and are often illegal. Textbooks are produced exclusively for classroom instruction and must be revised regularly to remain useful. A novel, poem, or play, however, is an author's own creation, irrespective of its use in a school setting. For this reason alone, expurgation or alteration of such works—including under the cover of "revision"—by anyone other than the author is impermissible in principle. Where applicable, it is a violation of copyright law.

Sometimes, however, before a work of fiction reaches the school it may be altered by a publisher who has reissued the work in an anthology or other educational format. The changes may "correct" or "update" colloquial language, or a text may be altered or deleted to satisfy perceived sensibilities, as has happened to Mark Twain and Shakespeare, to name but two. Often deletions or changes are not even indicated with ellipses or some other device. Such practices have come under increasing criticism. A committee of the National Council of Teachers of English has passed a resolution against all changes in texts.[18]

Of course, were educators to insist only on complete and uncut texts, students might be denied all exposure to certain lengthy or complicated works and, as a rule, anthologies would be excluded. Publishers will undoubtedly continue to release various editions of classic and other works of literature, and educators will choose from among these according to their specific situations and needs. Nevertheless, schools should be guided first and foremost by commitments to openness and accuracy. As the American Association of University Professors has declared:

> We can think of no reason that is consistent with any proper concept of education in a free society for expurgating a novel, play, or poem. Where literature is concerned, we can think of no reason why the classroom and school library should ever be other than what they seem, places where a work of fiction is as it appears to be. There is no reason why teachers and librarians should be induced to deceive their students, or why students should be misled as to the actual nature or content of what they are reading. Not only does deception have no place whatever in the school, but trimming a work of fiction to fit today's opinions is utterly reprehensible.[19]

Sexuality

The treatment of sexuality in our culture is a major issue that is also linked to concern with morality. Frank treatments of adolescent sexual awakening or of perceived sexual "deviancy" in literature are frequent targets of complaints. Sometimes the mere depiction of sexual behavior is thought to be synonymous with advocating that behavior. Although works of fiction assigned as classroom reading are not commonly devoted to sexual themes, many works of contemporary young adult literature found in school libraries by authors like Judy Blume, Robert Cormier, and Norma Klein treat this issue with considerable frankness.

One of Judy Blume's most controversial works is her novel, *Forever*, which deals with a young girl's emergence into womanhood and her difficult first explorations of the meaning of love. Certainly the book is not to every parent's taste. Blume herself has ruefully admitted that, if published today, *Forever* might be labeled an adult work.[20] Yet the book has been welcomed with enthusiasm by young readers, and many parents and educators applaud its sensitive and compassionate approach to complex adolescent problems.

One place where *Forever* became a target of censorship was Wyoming. A group of more than 36 parents called the book "pornographic" and said it would encourage readers "to experiment with sexual encounters." *Forever*, one father charged, "condones premarital sex in every way. The only thing it leaves out is pictures and, the way they go into some of this detail, you don't even need pictures. If that is educational, there's something wrong with the education system. . . . If there's more books like that in there, I say get them out," he threatened.

The school district followed its reconsideration policy, however, and *Forever* was retained in both junior and senior high school libraries. Moreover, at a public hearing support for the Blume book was widespread. Whereas 6 people signed up to speak for its removal, 41 signed up to defend its selection. Charles Levendosky, editorial page editor of the *Casper Star-Tribune*, told the committee,

> I think the most important issue here is not the issue of the selection of Judy Blume's book nor the views about what the book means. I think the issue here, the central issue, is whether a parent has the right to limit other children's right to read. . . . Mr. B___ has no right to limit the reading of my children or your children. It is at this juncture that Mr. B___ becomes a censor.[21]

A positive and practical suggestion, which could appropriately be directed to virtually all would-be school censors, was made by a Gillette, Wyoming, librarian. She advised those protesting *Forever* to

> . . . submit a list of books that more reflect their view of the themes of maturity and growth, send the list to the librarian, and ask that these books be considered for purchase. . . . Rather than depriving some people of materials they feel suitable for their children, a group who has different views on maturity and growth can help the library media staff to meet the criteria of providing a wide range of views on these topics for their child.[22]

Gay and Lesbian Literature

The development over the past two decades of the gay rights movement has begun, since about 1989, to have an impact on school
libraries and classrooms. Partly under the influence of external pressures and partly on their own initiative, many educators and librarians
have sought to accommodate the needs of both homosexual students
and pupils with gay or lesbian parents and to educate all students about
diverse sexual orientations in a spirit of tolerance and opposition to
discrimination. Much of the effort has focused on broadening sex education curricula (see below), but the emergence of specifically gay-
oriented literature for children and especially young adults and the
increasingly frank nature of other literature has challenged some
school districts.

Two young adult novels with a gay orientation, *Annie on My Mind*,
by Nancy Garden, and *All American Boys*, by Frank Mosca, were
donated in 1990 to three high school libraries in San Ramon, California, as part of a larger donation to all high schools in Contra Costa
County. But the books were seized from librarians by school administrators, who then "lost" them.[23] Whatever the merits or demerits of
these books may be, such actions amount to censorship, pure and
simple. Romantic literature about homosexual love should be judged
according to the same criteria as romantic literature about heterosexual love.

To be sure, no school library need accept any donated item. However, especially in light of budgetary constraints that compel growing
numbers of public schools to acquire much of their library holdings in
such a manner, districts should make clear that donated materials are
subject to the same selection criteria and procedures as purchased
materials. If such materials are *not* accepted they must be returned and
the donors informed of the decision and its rationale. For an administrator or librarian to short-circuit such policies and procedures through
any sort of unilateral action based on the personal opinion of a self-
appointed individual or group is impermissible—doubly so if done in
secret. In the San Ramon incident, the donor was charged not only with
censorship but with theft as well.

In 1991, Boston-based Alyson Publications initiated a series of
children's books oriented toward explanation of gay lifestyles for children of gay parents and other children, including *Daddy's Roommate*,
by Michael Willhoite and *Heather Has Two Mommies*, by Leslea
Newman. Efforts by public libraries to acquire titles in the series have
met with protests, almost all of which were unsuccessful. The books

can also be expected to attract attention in schools. In New York City, a community school board in Queens voted unanimously to reject a first-grade multicultural curriculum entitled "Children of the Rainbow" because its bibliography listed three Alyson titles. The books were not required of any student to read or teacher to teach, but were to be presented as resources.[24]

Sex Education

Treatment of sexuality and human reproduction sometimes poses a more difficult problem in required texts used in biology, health education, or similar classes. Here students are a "captive audience," and parental and community concerns about such controversial themes as teenage pregnancy, homosexuality, abortion and contraception, AIDS, and even masturbation may exert strong and contradictory pressures on teachers and administrators.

Although surveys show that more than 80 percent of the population supports sex education, a highly vocal minority objects not only to literary and artistic representations of sexuality, but also to more objective and factual discussions of this subject. Though consistently supported by an overwhelming majority of citizens, sex education classes are often targets of censorship efforts for going "too far" or for teaching "how to do it." Some who object to materials used in these classes actually oppose the inclusion of any kind of sex education in school curricula, even as elective courses. Two Florida textbook critics called their district's sex education program "a farce" and questioned its necessity, since "the nitty-gritty of it can be taught in less than an hour."[25]

Significant disagreements also remain about the permissible scope of sex education and about what students should be told. Some people believe that any instruction about how to use contraceptives or obtain an abortion will undermine traditional moral standards and parental efforts to encourage celibacy—even if birth control or abortion are not explicitly advocated, and even if they are directly discouraged. Others argue that to deny students such information is to make a farce of education.

In Santa Barbara, California, the president of a school PTA demanded the removal of a sex education video because it did not sufficiently promote abstinence.[26] Many sex education curricula now encourage "abstinence" as a method of birth control, and in some states promotion of abstinence is required. But many believe that, unless

state laws otherwise require, encouraging abstinence should not exclude the presentation of information about other forms of birth
control, abortion, or about sexuality in general.

Efforts to educate students about the dangers of AIDS have also led
to controversy. In Bremerton, Washington, a parent objected to AIDS
education in the textbook *Human Sexuality*, arguing that the term
"safe sex" is an oxymoron. "I don't believe this is necessary," she said. In
Atlanta, the same book was labeled "a 'how-to' book" that "promotes
promiscuity in a subtle way . . . , encourages breaking the law, and tears
down normal sexual barriers."[27]

Designing an appropriate sex education program is well beyond
the scope of this book. Each school district will have to structure its
program in light of local preferences and in accordance with state
guidelines. Districts should be aware, however, that virtually every
available textbook and library resource material treating human sexuality is likely to be found objectionable by someone in the community,
even if the sex education class is entirely elective.

In Mount Morris, Illinois, controversy erupted over the use of two
supplemental reading books, *What's Happening to My Body? Book
for Boys* and *What's Happening to My Body? Book for Girls*, in a
special program designed to help young people cope with growing up.
This program, which is sponsored nationwide by the Lions Clubs, also
came under fire in Michigan.[28] In south Florida a series of health
education books for small children was placed on elementary school
library restricted shelves after a parent and a minister objected to two
pages describing the reproductive process that allegedly "reinforce the
pornographic message on HBO and Cinemax."[29]

Recognizing that a majority of American parents support some
form of sex education, opponents have begun designing their own
curricula and these have been adopted in some schools. One such
program, called *Sex Respect*, was developed with federal grant money
and is in use in over 1,500 school districts nationwide. A series of
workbooks espousing "traditional values" and such unique concepts as
"secondary virginity," *Sex Respect* calls for sexually active teens to
abstain from future premarital relations and thus regain "virgin" status.

In Wisconsin, however, the American Civil Liberties Union challenged use of the curriculum as tantamount to discrimination based on
gender, marital status, sexual orientation, and religion. The curriculum,
the ACLU charged in a 1991 lawsuit, stereotypes boys as "sexual ag-
gressors" and girls as "virginity protectors," mischaracterizes AIDS as
nature's way of making "a statement on sexual behavior," and presents
two-parent heterosexual couples as "the sole model of a healthy, 'real'

family."[30] Supporters of *Sex Respect* and others were quick to accuse the ACLU of promoting censorship, but the organization noted that while public schools enjoy great latitude in making choices and teaching from a chosen perspective, they may not indoctrinate students in a parochial set of beliefs and they may not discriminate.

If sex education is offered, whether as an elective or as a unit within some other required course in health or biology, the same principles of accuracy, openness, and tolerance that govern the selection of learning materials in less controversial fields should be applied. Scientific truths should not be kept hidden out of deference to the religious or moral beliefs of community members, no matter how widespread and sincerely held those beliefs may be. Some parents, for instance, believe that masturbation is harmful and sinful and discourage their adolescent children from touching their sex organs. That is their parental right, which the school must respect. But this can in no way justify keeping from students the scientific truth that masturbation causes no physical harm, and that most experts believe its psychological consequences are, for the most part, benign.

Violence

Many people from diverse perspectives have noted that American culture sometimes seems to endorse a hypocritical moral standard that looks askance at representations of even the most timid sexuality, while freely permitting portrayals of murder and mayhem. In this light, many well-intended people have sought to purge school libraries and classrooms of violent imagery. Complaints that library or teaching materials are too violent or simply too "depressing" are increasing in number. Many are linked to complaints about sexuality or other issues, however, and those who offer these complaints are quite frequently more concerned about moral, religious, or even political issues than about violence.

In Fairfield, Ohio, some parents objected to a series of books called *Wizards, Warriors and You*, citing several examples of "violent deaths." The real issue, however, with which parents were concerned was the books' alleged "acceptance and involvement in occult practices." Complaints in numerous schools about the horror novels of Stephen King often focus on the books' violent episodes, although usually greater stress is placed on their sexual passages or the use by characters of profanity. In one Maryland county two school board members found novels about a girl who lived in a mental institution, the slave-era underground railroad, and the Nazi Holocaust against the Jews too violent and "depressing" for school use.[31]

The depiction of violence—and for that matter sexuality—in films is often a problem. Some schools have adopted a general policy that they will not show any film that is rated R, although, of course, most educational films are unrated. Sometimes books from which R-rated films have been made are also criticized, with parents demanding that the standards of the motion picture industry be applied to library books. This is, of course, unacceptable. As the American Library Association's "Statement on Labeling" declares, "Labeling is an attempt to prejudice attitudes and as such, it is a censor's tool." With respect to motion picture or other ratings systems created by private groups, the policy states: "For the library to adopt or enforce any of these private systems, to attach such ratings to library materials, to include them in bibliographic records, library catalogs, or other finding aids, or otherwise to endorse them would violate the Library Bill of Rights."[32]

"Secular Humanism" and "New Age"

In the 1980s the charge that library or teaching materials advocated the "religion" of "secular humanism" brought together a polyglot of more specific objections to materials generally thought to be too "liberal" or otherwise opposed to traditional religion and morality. After about 1987, when a major legal initiative by opponents of this philosophy failed, the turmoil subsided. Yet efforts to link what some people find morally objectionable to propagation of an allegedly anti-Christian religion have not ceased. Increasingly, opponents of some school and library materials charge that these promote occult or eastern religious practices or espouse a "New Age" doctrine that is religious in character.

What exactly constitutes secular humanism, New Age—or for that matter any occult faith or many other threatening "-isms"—has never been clear to those who do not share the fear of these creeds. Groups trying to remove instructional or library materials from public schools have cited the following practices and content as examples of secular humanist or New Age indoctrination: drug education, death education, values clarification, global education, the study of socialism, the theory of evolution, depictions of women as professionals, and the look-say method of teaching reading. "Globalism, humanism, socialism, feminism, illuminism, New Age, etc. are all the same animal: the differences are semantic and inconsequential," wrote one critic.[33]

Yet for some Americans the labels secular humanism and New Age now carry negative connotations equivalent to those more generally associated with words like "racism" and "sexism." Opponents of allegedly secular humanist or New Age materials have argued that use of such materials in public schools promotes religious belief in a manner violating the constitutional separation of church and state. Underlying this charge, however, is often a deep-seated and powerful fear for the status of their own religious faith that can verge on almost medieval paranoia, as evidenced in the following quote from a 1988 book:

> Our children have been at risk for decades now as Satan has worked The Plan, wielding his dark supernatural powers in unprecedented attack waves. His goal: to wipe out all vestiges of Christianity and the Bible from our schools and our culture and, by so doing, to win youth away from Christ.
>
> Atheism and Secular Humanism, though extremely successful, were only crude first attempts by the Devil. In the New Age movement and religion, Satan has latched on to something far more effective and more direct.[34]

In the 1980s conservative textbook critics Mel and Norma Gabler and their firm, Educational Research Analysts, maintained that humanism was declared a religion by the United States Supreme Court. In fact, the Supreme Court has not ruled one way or the other about the nature of secular humanism. However, a Court decision on a related but distinct issue did refer briefly to "secular humanism" in a footnote that read "Among religions in this country which do not teach what would generally be considered a belief in the existence of God are Buddhism, Taoism, Ethical Culture, Secular Humanism, and others."[35] A footnote in a later case also made brief reference to this note, but that is the full extent of the Supreme Court's commentary on the matter.

The first, and as yet only, court decision to define secular humanism as a religion was issued in Mobile, Alabama, in 1987 by U.S. District Court Judge W. Brevard Hand.[36] Judge Hand ruled that 44 social studies, history, and home economics textbooks be removed from Alabama's list of approved texts—and from the state's classrooms— because they promote "secular humanism." He was overruled six months later, and the fundamentalist Christians who brought the lawsuit decided not to seek review by the United States Supreme Court.

Judge Hand said the case was about "the allegedly improper promotion of certain religious beliefs." Secular humanism, he ruled, teaches "that moral choices are purely personal and can only be based on some autonomous, as yet undiscovered and unfulfilled, inner self." Moreover, according to Hand, the contested textbooks "discriminate against the very concept of religion and theistic religions in particular, by omissions so serious that a student learning history from them would not be apprised of relevant facts about America's history. . . . The texts reviewed are not merely bad history, but lack so many facts as to equal ideological promotion."

Many commentators on education agree that, in an effort to avoid controversy, many widely used history and social studies textbooks lack adequate discussions of religion in American life. But Hand's notion that an *absence* of information on this subject constitutes "ideological promotion" of a secular faith was extraordinary. Who is to determine which facts are "relevant," and how many of these must be mentioned to constitute fair treatment? It is bad enough for a court to label books "secular humanist" because of what they say, but it is patently absurd for any court—or private censors—to seek to ban books because of what they *don't* say.

Those who have levied the charge that secular humanism is being promoted in the schools often seem to believe that educators are especially active in the humanist movement. Of course, that some influential educators like John Dewey have called themselves humanists should by no means suggest that all or even most educators today embrace such a creed. In fact, nearly 80 percent of American educators are members of a church or synagogue, and approximately 60 percent say they attend religious services weekly.[37]

No matter which religion educators espouse, however, the First Amendment requires public schools to remain *neutral* on the subject of religion. Most teachers and administrators take their obligation to uphold the Constitution very seriously. Those who charge that public school students are being unconstitutionally indoctrinated in secular humanist or New Age religious precepts usually oppose Supreme Court rulings that have removed familiar religious practices such as prayer and Bible readings from the schools. This suggests that the real concern motivating these critics is not their opposition to the illegal establishment of a "religion," but instead their desire that students exercise more traditional religious and moral beliefs that the would-be censors themselves espouse.

When charges of promoting "secular humanism" or the "New Age" are made against library or instructional materials, those making the charges should be compelled to define their terms and to specify precisely how challenged materials promote these beliefs. More often than not, complainants are not really aroused by the supposedly "religious" content of the challenged material but by the material's perceived moral, cultural, or political impact.

Witchcraft and the Occult

It may surprise some educators to learn that probably the most hotly contested issue today is the charge that instructional or library materials promote witchcraft, Satanism or simply a harmful interest in the occult. In the 1987 AASA survey a greater number of districts reported complaints about witchcraft and the occult than reported complaints about "secular humanism." All indications are that the number of such complaints has continued to rise, perhaps even exceeding complaints about profanity.

Objections to witchcraft and the occult have come to resemble previous complaints about secular humanism. Definitions of "witchcraft" are expanded to include the most diverse practices and beliefs. Materials treating witchcraft have been found by some to promote not only blasphemy but also obscenity, political radicalism, and the teaching of evolution. Some complainants identify any teaching *about* non-Western religious traditions or *about* mythology with the teaching *of* witchcraft. As in the secular humanism and New Age issues, the argument is increasingly heard that schools are violating the First Amendment's establishment clause by promoting Satanic religious beliefs.

As a rule, these objections are not made in the name of rationalism and science—for instance, there have been few challenges to works about astrology as scientifically bogus. Instead, those who object to materials on the grounds that they promote witchcraft do so generally on religious grounds. Sometimes, they believe that devils and witches are a real and active force for evil in the world that must be combated. "It's not fantasy, it's true," declared one upstate New York woman who sought the removal of *Meet the Werewolf* from an elementary school library.[38] More often, the charge of promoting witchcraft is used as a grab bag for a variety of complaints arising from a perceived decline in religious influence on education.

The issue has been further complicated by the emergence of small groups of self-declared "witches," who claim to practice a pre-Christian pagan religion. These groups have begun to defend their rights to religious expression against critics of the occult. In a San Francisco suburb, for example, a self-proclaimed witch who "came out of the broom closet" demanded that a school district ban the fairy tale "Hansel and Gretel" because it teaches children that it is acceptable to kill witches. "They would not use a story that would put any other religion in a light like this," she said.[39]

In many cases, traditional children's stories and Halloween tales have come under attack, including quite a few picture books for pre-schoolers with titles like *Witches, Witches, Witches* and *Witch Baby*. In Gilbert, Arizona, nine elementary school library books with "scary" themes of witchcraft and Halloween were challenged by an outraged parent. "What I'm fighting is that this is a religion like God is a religion and they're taking books on prayer out of the library. Some of these books explain satanic rituals and make them sound like fun," the parent said. She charged, for instance, that a picture book called *Witches, Pumpkins and Grinning Ghosts* "interests little minds into accepting the devil with all his evil works."[40]

Also frequently targeted for their allegedly occult content are juvenile and young adult novels with supernatural themes, including almost any novel by Stephen King. More significantly, perhaps, objections have been raised about library materials and curricula that highlight all sorts of folk literature, mythology, or comparative religion. In Nebraska, a book of Scandinavian mythology and another of folk tales from around the world were removed from a school library by a school board's "Americanism committee" after a parent complained they promote witchcraft. In Colorado, a world literature course segment on Greek and Roman mythology was challenged as "a misleading way to get kids' eyes on gods other than the almighty God."[41]

Materials that make even the slightest reference to nonwestern religious traditions have often been bracketed with more explicitly supernatural works. An Oregon school board rejected a supplemental health book that mentioned yoga and transcendental meditation. "My objection was that the school board, under the guise of wellness, was importing a form of eastern religious practices," said one of three parents who challenged the book. "If you're going to have an opening for eastern religious practices, you should have space for Christian religious practices too." *Wellness: Stress Management* was part of a series of supplemental readings for high school students that teachers had planned to place in the library. It was never proposed as required reading.[42]

In September 1992, a U.S. District Court Judge in Pennsylvania ruled that *Dragonwings*, a novel about a Chinese aviator, did not violate the First Amendment's prohibition against the establishment of religion. A church elder claimed that the book advanced the particular religions and beliefs of Taoism and reincarnation. It also allegedly promoted secular humanism by implying that man can achieve his goals without God's intervention. "The fact that religions and religious concepts are mentioned in school does not automatically constitute a violation of the establishment clause," the court declared. Beyond that, the book was used for a "purely secular purpose" and did not foster excessive state entanglement with religion. "In fact, little, if any, discussion of the book's religious references took place and when it did, the teachers were completely neutral on the matter. Neither the book nor the teachers who taught it expounded a particular religion as the only correct belief or even the preferred belief," the judge concluded.[43]

Opponents of witchcraft and the occult have also focused on curricular and extracurricular learning activities, including drug prevention and self-esteem programs. One such program, *Pumsy in Pursuit of Excellence,* asks young children to follow the adventures of Pumsy the dragon and her friend through various situations and feelings. The program is intended to teach children to make sound decisions, manage conflict, understand consequences, and gain self-respect. According to critics, however, the program attempts to teach these values by promoting "New Age religion, meditation and hypnosis." In numerous instances the simple fact that the program uses the supernatural image of a dragon was enough to draw criticism.[44]

In the 1980s, a special target of concern for many complainants was the game "Dungeons and Dragons," which has been popular among some teenagers and has sometimes been used by teachers and librarians as a supplementary educational tool. Opponents of the game charge that those who play it are not only exposed to satanic influences, but become obsessively involved in the activity. They claim that in several cases playing the game has led to suicide.

However, the mother of one 13-year-old player who took his own life spoke against an effort in Connecticut to ban the game. She said, "It was not from any game that my son committed suicide. Not even Dungeons and Dragons. . . . I think it is a tragedy how a certain group of people can take a tragic death and use it for their own purpose. . . . To take this game out of school is wrong. If the families don't want their children to play, then notify the school and request it."[45]

Although objections to secular humanism and New Age religion will undoubtedly continue to be heard, the increasing frequency of complaints about witchcraft suggests that this rubric offers would-be censors a more powerful mobilizing rationale for attacking the broad array of concerns that have been subsumed under the humanist and New Age labels. After all, the charge that secular humanists and New Agers are perverting children's minds is consistent with the long-standing tradition of "witch hunting" that is one of the more unattractive features of our political culture. But to tell an audience that secular humanism and New Age are alien religions coming into the schools to replace Christianity, one has first to explain what these religions are. This has the advantage that they can then be made into anything the would-be censor wants; but it has the disadvantage of being too abstract. Insofar as there are identifiable secular humanists, for instance, they are of varied religious faiths and some have no religion at all. By contrast, adherents of occult religions may be few in number, but they are readily identified with a traditionally "dangerous" creed.

Why do some people actually believe and fear that children are learning to be witches and Satanists in our public schools? The appeal, of course, is first and foremost to fear. There is a fear of difference, and, it must be noted, a fear of women, too. Concern with witchcraft has historically been associated with male fears of women and with concern among some males and females about the power of "emancipated women" in society.

The concern with witchcraft and the occult is also a reaction to the loss of control that many people feel in their lives. Popular censors often act because they fear ideas and images that are beyond their control. Opponents of occult-oriented literature have, in many instances, turned to venerable cultural traditions for an explanation. The world is out of control because Satan—and human satanists—manipulate it.

The *Impressions* Controversy

Undoubtedly the work most censored on the basis of its alleged promotion of Satanism, witchcraft or New Age religion is the elementary school reading series *Impressions*, since about 1990 probably the single most popular target of public school censorship throughout the country. According to People for the American Way, in 1990–91 *Impressions* was challenged in at least 45 jurisdictions. Produced originally in Canada, the literature-based series comprises fifteen books, including 822 selections from novels, poetry, drama, biographies, short stories, folklore, fantasy, and other forms of literature, and is used in more than 1,500 schools in 34 states. *Impressions* features contributions from such authors as Martin Luther King, Jr., Maurice Sendak, Rudyard Kipling, Laura Ingalls Wilder, A. A. Milne, Madeleine L'Engle, C. S. Lewis, and Dr. Seuss.[46]

The first cited controversies over *Impressions* came in Washington and Oregon in 1987, where objectors focused on alleged "overtones of witchcraft, mysticism and fantasy" and "persistent themes of rebellion against parents and authority figures." Others argued that the series was "depressing" and "violent." The objections in these first incidents, and in most thereafter, focused on only a quite small portion of the material in the series—only 22 of the 822 selections deal with ghosts, goblins, or witches. But here, as in subsequent incidents, those who objected generally sought a complete ban on all the *Impressions* volumes.

The controversy over *Impressions* escalated dramatically after a conservative Christian periodical published the first of several blistering attacks on the series in September 1990, and the journal's sponsoring group began a concerted mobilization effort. In almost all instances, *Impressions* challengers complained that the series promoted Satanism, the occult, and New Age religion. Challengers, for instance, cited pictures of rainbows in the books' illustrations, asserting that the rainbow was a New Age religious symbol. Elsewhere charges were made that cats in the books' stories suggested a preoccupation with the occult.

The controversy developed initially on the west coast, especially after California state education authorities adopted the book in 1989, but has since spread to urban, suburban, and rural districts across the country, with particular hotbeds in Alaska, California, Illinois, Maryland, and South Dakota. In 1991–92 the battle over *Impressions* entered the legal system. In a case that was watched closely by educators and religious interests, United States District Court Judge William Shoob in Sacramento, California, on April 2, 1992, dismissed a suit charging that the series violated the U.S. and California constitutions by promoting the "religions of witchcraft and neopaganism."

Initially, the suit, filed with the support of the Rev. Donald Wildmon's American Family Association by two fundamentalist Christians from Woodland, California, charged broadly that the series was too morbid, displayed disrespect toward parents, and that there were too many references in it to witches and goblins. Later, however, the grounds were narrowed to allegations that 38 stories, poems, and supplementary activities recommended in teacher's manuals promoted witchcraft and neopaganism.

"There is no constitutional basis," Judge Shoob wrote, "for the court to order that the activities in question be excluded from the classroom simply because isolated instances of those activities may happen to coincide or harmonize with the tenets of two relatively obscure religions."[47] Similar conclusions were reached in two suits filed in United States District Court in Illinois.

Creationism

The question of church and state is also integral to the debate over the teaching of evolution and so-called "creation science" in the schools, which has waxed and waned in American education for much of this century. Although the controversy has abated somewhat from the intense level of the early and mid-1980s, objections continue to be raised against materials that allegedly promote evolutionary "theory" as science. Advocates of "creationism" have been distinguished from other critics of instructional and library materials by their efforts to *add* materials to the curriculum that reflect their own views—views that most scientists believe are religiously based. Still, attempts to give "equal time" to creationist theories retain many of the hallmarks of a censorship effort.

In 1968, the United States Supreme Court ruled in *Epperson* v. *Arkansas* that teaching the Darwinian theory of evolution cannot be prohibited on the grounds that it runs counter to Christian religious belief about the origin of man.[48] In *Edwards* v. *Aguillard*, decided in June 1987, the high court further ruled that a Louisiana law requiring that teaching of evolution be "balanced" with teaching of "creation science" was unconstitutional on the grounds that the law lacked a clear secular purpose.[49]

Some legal experts believe that a constitutionally acceptable formula for teaching *about* creation beliefs could be found, but they doubt this would satisfy creationists. "If, as creationists maintain, creationist theory deserves inclusion in science classes for intellectual reasons, then it too must be verified by conventional scientific methods," wrote one theorist.[50] Only a tiny handful of scientists, however, believe that creationism is true science. The overwhelming majority of biologists treat evolution as fact, not theory. What is "theoretical" (but also accepted by the great majority of scientists) is the Darwinian explanation of evolution by means of natural selection. The National Academy of the Sciences likened the introduction of "creation science" into school science courses to "requiring the teaching of Ptolemaic [pre-Copernican] astronomy or pre-Columbian geography."[51]

For 10 years, the Texas State Board of Education required all textbooks that treat the theory of evolution to "identify it as only one of several explanations of the origins of mankind and avoid limiting young people in their search for meaning of their human existence." Also, each textbook that treats evolution "must carry a statement on the introductory page that any material included in the book is clearly presented as theory rather than fact."[52]

"In effect," concluded the American Association of University Professors,

> The Texas rule encumbered educators in the schools in teaching that which is generally regarded by the scientific community as integral to scientific knowledge and understanding, and what the vast majority of Texas teachers no doubt understood to be the scientific truth about the origins of life. Teachers, in exercising their professional judgment, could have used supplementary materials to provide their students with a deeper understanding of evolution than that suggested by the truncated textbook. But the required use of the textbook would then have presented teachers with a repugnant choice. If they adhered to the admonition in the textbook concerning evolution, their teaching would not have reflected the best professional standards. On the other hand, if they taught biological evolution as a validated scientific hypothesis that is at the heart of all modern research into human evolution, they presumably would have been subject to some institutional sanction for failure to perform professional duties.
>
> The Texas experience suggests that changes in textbooks that contradict longstanding tenets of inquiry and understanding in a particular field of knowledge . . . or that are meant to advance, or have the effect of advancing, a religious belief, can seriously encroach upon freedom in the schools.[53]

Some believe it may, in the end, be educationally reasonable and constitutionally acceptable to excuse some students from discussions of evolution in deference to the sincerely held religious beliefs of their families. In any event, efforts that effectively seek to limit the teaching of up-to-date scientific knowledge about the descent and development of the human species amount to a form of censorship.

Racism and Sexism

Increasing awareness over the past several decades of the rights and sensitivities of minorities and of women has resulted in, among other things, heightened efforts to remove racial and sexual stereotypes and insults from educational materials. Overwhelmingly, educators and the general public have welcomed and embraced these efforts, and considerable progress has been made. Contemporary curricula are far from perfect; but the sensitivity of instructional and library materials to the legitimate concerns of minority groups, and the commitment of these materials to ethnic and sexual equality and to pluralism, certainly run deeper than ever before in our history.

Unfortunately, however, requests to remove materials that may be construed as racist or sexist can pose a difficult dilemma for school librarians. Although, as noted in chapter 2, the school library's mission is not exactly the same as that of the public library, its commitment to making available alternative views and ideas should be no less firm. Racial, sexual, and other prejudices are part of our country's history and of its present reality. The school library will necessarily reflect this, which is not wholly a bad thing since students can hardly be taught to identify and reject prejudicial thought without directly confronting examples of bias and stereotyping.

Nevertheless, occasionally members of a group that has been a target of bigotry or oppression will seek to limit access to works which they believe help to maintain or further that bigotry and oppression. The problem is not generally great when it comes to openly derogatory materials. These are not often found in school libraries and are mostly used in classroom instruction strictly as "negative examples." More frequently, conflict arises when a work that most people believe opposes bigotry is understood by some critics quite differently. They may seek to impose an extreme or idiosyncratic definition of prejudicial material on the schools. Or they may judge a work solely on the basis of its use of inflammatory language, with little concern for overall message or context.

Members of oppressed and minority groups also rarely speak with a single voice. Where some find certain materials insulting, others in the group find these very works liberating. For instance, some members of the black community find black feminist Alice Walker's Pulitzer Prize-winning novel *The Color Purple* insulting to black men. They are also often offended by the novel's lesbian theme which, it is sometimes argued, would never be accepted for school use if the characters in the book were white. Black parents have objected to the book on these grounds in California and North Carolina. The majority of black and white educators, however, praise the book.

Among the works whose presence in school libraries or use in the classroom have been challenged as prejudiced or stereotypical of some group are Shakespeare's *Merchant of Venice*, which some Jewish organizations have accused of anti-semitism; Mario Puzo's *The Godfather*, which drew fire from some Italian-Americans; and Harper Lee's novel, *To Kill a Mockingbird*, which some black groups claim is racist.

In 1984, a group of black educators called for a ban on classroom use of any book employing the word "nigger," regardless of context and intent.[54] Since then, complaints about books with the word have increased. Probably the most frequent target has been Mark Twain's *The Adventures of Huckleberry Finn*, but other widely praised classics have been criticized on these grounds. In Modesto, California, a parent and local NAACP official asked the school board to remove John Stein-beck's *Of Mice and Men*—a frequent target of those upset by profanity—from a reading list because of its use of the word.[55]

The issue of sexism can be especially frustrating for school systems because the role of women in American society continues to change dramatically. In response to these changes there have been complaints against textbooks and library materials that promote both traditional and newer female roles. Various nursery rhymes and children's stories, which some feminists say promote negative images of women, have come under fire, while elsewhere conservative women's organizations have objected to reading textbooks that portray women as profession-als or skilled workers. They sometimes have argued that these denigrate the contributions of housewives and others who do more traditional women's work.

Of course such complaints—indeed, all complaints—should be handled with sensitivity. After all, it can hardly be said that all contem-porary textbooks—not to mention works of literature—are free of prejudicial stereotyping, and most school selection policies and the laws of many states mandate the elimination of recognized bias, if not from the library then certainly from the classroom. Still, materials charged with racism or sexism need not, fundamentally, be treated in a manner different from those accused of secular humanism or witch-craft. As a rule, no matter how sympathetic or unsympathetic an educator may be with the fundamental goals and values of those who protest, materials that meet selection criteria should be retained and those that do not should be removed.

The Case of Huck Finn

In recent years the issue of racism has been sharply focused on prob-lems raised by use of the highly charged word "nigger." It should (but, unfortunately, cannot) go without saying that "nigger" is now and has always been a vile racist epithet. No reasonable argument can be made for schools presenting this word in some sort of "neutral" or "value-free" manner. Having stressed this, however, it must be recognized that the word appears in a variety of contexts in a number of important and traditionally studied works of literature, including several whose over-all message favors racial equality and tolerance.

Mark Twain's classic novel, *The Adventures of Huckleberry Finn*, and its character Nigger Jim provide a case in point that has become a major focus of controversy. A growing number of African-American parents, civil rights activists, and educators have called for an end to the teaching of this book in English classes, and a few have even demanded its removal from school libraries. Most educators, however, black and white, have resisted these requests.

That *Huckleberry Finn* belongs in just about every school library in America is generally accepted. When it comes to classroom instruction, however, the issue is not so simple. To be sure, sophisticated readers of the novel quickly perceive that Twain's message is one of tolerance, and that Nigger Jim is one of the few positive characters that Huck meets in his travels. It is precisely because Huck and Jim transcend race that they have become symbols for the outcast—by choice and by compulsion—in American culture. Students, however, are generally not yet sophisticated readers, and if these messages are not communicated to them explicitly by the teacher, it is argued, the awesome power of "nigger" may burn a very different message on their minds. As the novel's opponents point out, there are many classic American works conveying similar themes that could easily replace Twain.

Critics of *Huckleberry Finn* often point to the especially uncomfortable position of African-American students in classes that are predominantly white. Incidents can certainly be documented where African-American students have been compelled against their will to read the part of Nigger Jim, while their classmates snickered about the character's dialect; or where other instances of a teacher's insensitivity to the feelings evoked by the word "nigger" led to embarrassment or insult. It might further be pointed out that even greater problems may be associated with teaching the book in classes with no minority students, where the racial issues in the book may be avoided, allowing prejudice to go unchallenged. However, the inability of some teachers to address the problem of racism with compassion and insight is one matter, blaming a book for this serious educational problem is quite another.

Professor Jocelyn Chadwick-Joshua of the University of North Texas, an African-American, has campaigned to keep *Huckleberry Finn* in school curricula. When she first taught the novel to eleventh graders nearly two decades ago, however, she thought differently. "I was hung up on the word 'nigger,'" she said. But after learning about Twain, an abolitionist who paid the bills for one of the first African-American students to graduate from Yale Law School, she concluded that the book is a satirical attack on the hypocrisy of racism. "It's antiracist," she concluded.

"It is a problem for minorities to read works that are sensitive like that," she acknowledged. "But it makes the race strong. It makes us aware, culturally aware, of where we've come from." She stresses that preparation is key. "If you're going to teach that kind of work, students need to know the history before they begin the actual reading. Otherwise, they just don't get it." [56]

It is not the purpose of this book to recommend or not recommend the teaching of *Huckleberry Finn* or any other specific work. That the book *can* be taught to both white and black students in a manner that develops the students' appreciation of racial equality as well as of literature is incontestable. Whether every school or teacher is in a position to do this, however, may not always be so clear. Whatever the case, the decision should be made by the local school district on the basis of a thorough consideration and discussion, according to appropriate policies and procedures, of the educational merits and demerits of teaching this or any other book, and not in response to censorship pressures exerted on the school.

Those who oppose the teaching of *Huckleberry Finn* or other allegedly racist or sexist materials, no more nor less than those who oppose use of books on the occult or works of literature with frank depictions of sexuality, have every right to participate in and contribute to the selection process. What they may *not* do is impose their views in ways that prevent the schools from fulfilling their mission of educating youth in the democratic spirit of *both* decision by majority vote and tolerance of and respect for minority opinions and values.

4

Establishing Selection Policies

The integrity of the process of professional teachers making professional judgments in the selection of educational resources is protected against threats of censorship by having a school board which believes in resisting censorship and in supporting the Bill of Rights.

Minnesota Civil Liberties Union[1]

Many challenges to academic freedom go unchecked or are mishandled simply because preparations have not been made for an effective response. An arsenal of defenses must be available to the school at the moment a confrontation begins with a would-be censor. Every school system should, therefore, have a comprehensive written policy on the selection of all instructional and library materials—including textbooks, library books, periodicals, films, videotapes, and recordings. A materials selection policy will help define and promote the educational goals of the school. It also will serve as a defense against censorship efforts.

A written policy is essential for three main reasons. First, haphazard patterns of acquisition are unprofessional and result in waste. Materials may overlap in content or may be unrelated to changing patterns of instruction.

Second, a written policy encourages stability and continuity. Staff may come and go, but the policy and procedures manual, kept up-to-date, will help assure smooth transitions when organizational changes occur.

Finally, ambiguity and confusion are far less likely to result if a school's policies are set down clearly and concisely for all to see. A comprehensive policy on the selection of instructional and library materials assists school professionals in rationally explaining the school program to the community. In a crisis, when there are complaints about social studies texts, human development materials, or works of fiction in the library or classroom, the use of the "objectionable" item can be justified and explained in accordance with general principles established by the school system.

Who Makes Policy?

Good selection policies and procedures will be formulated with input from a wide variety of sources. Depending upon the size and nature of the school system, policies may exist at several levels. There may be a district policy setting overall guidelines and a school policy that adapts district rules to a specific educational situation. Within a school, especially a large one, the librarian may enjoy a certain degree of autonomy in working out policies and procedures, as may individual departments.

Although those preparing policies and procedures should welcome participation by citizen groups, parents, and students, responsibility for the selection and reconsideration of instructional and library materials lies ultimately with the school board and, more immediately, with the school district's professional staff. The school board will receive input from the community regarding courses to be made available, and it has the right and the responsibility to set guidelines for adopting school courses, reevaluating the content of those courses, and formulating a due process procedure for handling complaints from the community. The school board ultimately has the responsibility to resolve controversial matters that cannot be worked out between the professional staff and the community.

It should be stressed, however, that legal precedents establish that school board members do not have the right to impose "narrowly partisan or political" beliefs and biases on the district, even where these biases may reflect majority views (see chapter 6). As Supreme Court Justice William J. Brennan, Jr., has written, "Our Constitution does not permit the official suppression of *ideas*." However, the Supreme Court has ruled that school boards may restrict literature that is "pervasively vulgar" (the Court offered no definition of this term) or educationally unsuitable.[2]

Although the school board's responsibility is to establish guidelines, leaving elaboration and implementation to staff, board members are also obliged to stay in regular contact with district professionals; keep informed about selection decisions and potential conflicts; and offer systematic guidance, where appropriate. How this is done may vary from district to district. A single board member may be assigned special responsibilities in the area of materials selection, or there may be a standing committee, perhaps composed of board members, administrators, and instructional and library staff, responsible for regular oversight of resources and teaching methods. Often lists of books and other materials are submitted to boards for a vote, sometimes after a period during which these are made available to board members and the public for inspection.

In no event, however, should the full board be kept in the dark, intentionally or inadvertently, about how materials are selected, about what kinds of materials are being used and, most important, about the principles governing selection policy—including the professional principles of academic and intellectual freedom. Establishing avenues of communication and familiarizing board members with selection criteria and procedures and with library and classroom materials only in the midst of a crisis will not be conducive to effective conflict resolution.

School professionals have the primary responsibility to determine the content of courses offered by the school district and to select appropriate teaching methods and educational resources. Teachers and librarians should work closely with administrators and school board members in formulating, revising, and implementing all selection policies and procedures. In most instances, policies will be developed or revised by teachers and librarians and referred to administrators and the board for approval or, if necessary, amendment. School board approval may be critical to giving the policy statement legal force.

At the request of the principal or district administration, teachers and librarians have the responsibility to explain and clarify to the public any courses offered by the school district. The professional staff also has the responsibility to respond to complaints and to justify their choices of educational resources and teaching methods. They too, however, do not have the right to impose personal, political, religious, social, or aesthetic beliefs or biases on their students.

Basic Components of a Selection Policy

A materials selection statement should be positive.[3] It should be a viable, working document that relates to concrete, everyday practices and problems. The statement should, in effect:

AASA Resolution Supports Academic Freedom

For a number of years, the American Association of School Adminis-trators has gone on record to stress the importance of schools doing their part to uphold academic freedom. Its 1988 resolution stated:

AASA is concerned about indiscriminate, arbitrary, and/or capricious efforts to censor and limit academic freedom. AASA urges school boards to adopt appropriate policy for the selection, evaluation, and removal of instructional materials.

- Provide a plan for strengthening the breadth and depth of library and media center collections and of the instructional program.
- Provide adequate detail to give clear guidance to individual staff members.
- Be general enough to offer the flexibility necessary for creative and imaginative educational decision making.

The policy statement should, of course, comply with and take note of any and all state laws governing school textbook and instructional materials selection policy. Where appropriate, the statement may re-produce relevant excerpts from applicable statutes or code.

The policy statement should be clearly written and avoid jargon. It should be understandable and accessible to members of the commu-nity. Although the length of the statement will depend in great measure on the size and complexity of the district it is intended to serve, as a rule excess verbiage should be avoided. Long and rambling policy state-ments are not only unwieldy, they tend to be forgotten.

An effective written materials selection policy will include the following six components:

- A brief discussion of the *philosophy and objectives* for the selec-tion of educational resources in the district or school.
- A statement delegating *responsibilities* for the selection of mate-rials to appropriate professional school personnel (e.g., teachers representing various departments and grade levels and librarians).
- A statement delineating specific *criteria* to be used in the selection of instructional and library materials and teaching methods.
- A step-by-step description of selection *procedures* from initial screening to final selection.

- A section directly addressing problems associated with the acquisition of *controversial materials*, including statements in support of academic and intellectual freedom and opposing censorship.
- A clear statement of procedures for *review of challenged materials* and for community and parental input. Each specific step to be taken when a request for reconsideration is made, and all possible avenues of appeal, should be listed.

Objectives

A good materials selection statement will elucidate in succinct terms what the schools are trying to accomplish in their program of services and the specific objectives in given areas of service. The overarching goal may be expressed in the broadest terms. For example, for the district as a whole, the policy may state:

> Instructional materials are selected by the school district to implement, enrich, and support the educational program for the student. Materials must serve both the breadth of the curriculum and the needs and interests of individual students. It is the obligation of the district to provide for a wide range of abilities and to respect the diversity of many differing points of view. To this end, principles must be placed above personal opinion and reason above prejudice in the selection of materials of the highest quality and appropriateness.

For the library or media center the statement may declare that its main objective is "to provide the students with a wide range of educational materials that will enrich and support the curriculum and meet the needs of students and faculty." This may then be broken down to more specific objectives such as providing background materials to supplement classroom instruction, to provide access to classics of American and world literature, or to provide a broad range of materials on current issues of controversy to help students develop critical analytic skills. It may also be noted that the library's philosophy is "to provide resources on all levels of difficulty, with diversity of appeal, allowing for the presentation of many different points of view."

The objectives for selection should reflect the specific goals of the instructional program. In the case of textbooks, the goals may vary from subject to subject. For example, in the sciences, one principal goal might be accuracy in terms of the latest scientific knowledge; while in history, diversity and balance in the presentation of conflicting points of view might be emphasized.

Responsibility for Selection

The policy will precisely define responsibility for selection of all types of materials. It will name by professional position those persons responsible in each area of selection. Since, in most states, the locally elected or appointed school board has, by law, broad powers and responsibility in the selection of instructional materials, this responsibility should be explicitly delegated in policy to appropriate professionals. The policy should state *exactly* who is responsible for selection of specified types of materials. Avenues of communication between professionals and the board and procedures for involving all parties, including the board, should be indicated in general terms.

While selection of materials involves many people, including administrators, supervisors, teachers, library media specialists, students, and community residents, the responsibility for coordinating and recommending the selection and purchase of library media materials should rest with certificated library media personnel. Responsibility for coordinating the selection and purchase of textbooks and other classroom materials may rest with appropriate department chairs, textbook evaluation committees, or curriculum specialists. Teachers should retain some flexibility to choose for their own classes supplementary materials and, in some instances, textbooks—in accordance with criteria and procedures established in policy.

Sample Statement of Responsibility

Here is a sample statement of responsibility for a district:

The Board of Education will delegate to the Superintendent the authority and responsibility for selection of all print and nonprint materials. Responsibilities for actual selection will rest with appropriate professionally trained personnel who shall discharge this obligation consistent with the Board's adopted selection criteria and procedures. Selection procedures will involve representatives of the professional staff directly affected by the selections, and persons qualified by preparation to aid in wise selection.

Such a statement should be followed by more detailed statements of responsibility for selection of basal textbooks, supplementary classroom materials, and library and media center resources.

Criteria

In terms of subject matter covered, the policy must include selection criteria, and the application of criteria, relevant to the various objectives stated previously in the policy. These will include artistic or literary excellence, appropriateness to level of user, authenticity, interest, cost, and circumstances of use. Technical criteria, such as clarity of sound in audio materials, can be included as well. Although specific criteria to be used in the evaluation of potentially controversial materials should be fully elaborated in a special section, the overall treatment of selection criteria should include statements indicating how the school puts into practice its commitments to diversity and tolerance.

It may be advisable in many instances to list both general and more specific selection criteria. A statement of general selection criteria might include the following:

Instructional and library materials will be selected according to the following criteria as they apply.

1. Learning resources will support and be consistent with the general educational goals of the state and district and the aims and objectives of individual schools and specific courses.
2. Learning resources will meet high standards of quality in factual content and presentation.
3. Learning resources will be appropriate for the subject area and for the age, emotional development, ability level, learning styles, and social development of the students for whom the materials are selected.
4. Physical format and appearance of learning resources will be suitable for their intended use.
5. Learning resources will be designed to help students gain an awareness of our diverse society.
6. Learning resources will be designed to motivate students and staff to examine their own attitudes and behaviors and to comprehend their own duties, responsibilities, rights, and privileges as participating citizens in our society.
7. Learning resources will be selected for their strengths, rather than rejected for their weaknesses.
8. The selection of learning resources on controversial issues will be directed toward maintaining a balanced collection representing various views.
9. Learning resources will clarify historical and contemporary forces

by presenting and analyzing intergroup tension and conflict objectively, placing emphasis on recognizing and understanding social and economic problems.

To guide the professional staff with responsibility for selection, and to minimize the arbitrary and personal element that inevitably invades even the most carefully structured selection process, criteria should also be spelled out as specifically as possible for each type of material selected.

Among specific criteria that may be listed in the policy are:

- Educational significance.
- Contribution the subject matter makes to the curriculum and to the interests of the students.
- Favorable reviews found in standard selection sources.
- Favorable recommendations based on preview and examination of materials by professional personnel.
- Reputation and significance of the author, producer, or publisher.
- Validity, up-to-dateness, and appropriateness of material.
- Contribution the material makes to breadth of representative viewpoints.
- High degree of potential user appeal.
- High artistic quality and/or literary style.
- Quality and variety of format.
- Value commensurate with cost and/or need.
- Timeliness or permanence.
- Integrity.

Bibliographies, review journals, and other selection aids to be consulted should be listed by name.

Procedures

The policy statement should describe all steps in the selection process from initial screening to final selection. The purpose of this section of the policy statement is not only to indicate to responsible staff how criteria are to be applied, but also to clarify to community members how the school goes about acquiring instructional and library materials.

Procedures should provide clear and effective mechanisms for coordination among departments and professional staff; for handling recommendations from faculty, students, parents, and community groups; and for the ongoing review of existing materials for replacement due to wear and tear, supersession by more up-to-date works, and so forth. Any special procedures pertinent to library collection development or classroom materials acquisition should be spelled out. If specific selection aids were not listed in the previous section of the policy, a statement indicating that those responsible for selection will consult reputable reviewing sources would be appropriate here. The statement should include at least a partial list of approved selection aids. In some cases, it may also be advisable to list review sources that are not to be used.

The statement should note that gifts donated to the school library or media collection, or items submitted to the school for free distribution in class as educational materials, will be judged according to the same criteria as materials purchased by the school district. The statement might also explain any procedure whereby guest speakers will be granted permission to address individual classes or larger groups of students or faculty.

Controversial Materials

The policy should directly address problems associated with the acquisition of potentially controversial materials. The document should include here a statement on academic freedom and the importance of diversity, pluralism, and tolerance in a democratic society. This is the appropriate place to emphasize, in the most sweeping manner, the district's commitment to oppose censorship. The rights and responsibilities of both teachers and students to discuss and consider controversial issues in an atmosphere free from bias and prejudice should be delineated.

With respect to libraries and media centers, the policy should specifically endorse the ALA Library Bill of Rights by including in the text a statement that might read: "The school system subscribes in principle to the statements of policy on library philosophy as expressed in the American Library Association Library Bill of Rights, a copy of which is appended to and made an integral part of this policy." (Many existing district selection policies include endorsement of the 1969 AASL School Library Bill of Rights. This document has been superseded by the broader Library Bill of Rights, and selection policies should be amended to reflect this fact.) The statement might also endorse and even include the texts of some other relevant policy statements by national education organizations.

Although the selection policy should mainly steer away from efforts to formulate distinct policy principles with regard to current and specific areas of controversy, some districts have found it useful to include in their selection policies statements concerning racism and sexism or vulgar language in classroom and library materials. A simple statement that profanity, "dirty" words, or sexually oriented subject matter do not in themselves constitute grounds for exclusion may be useful and appropriate. Beyond this, however, statements about areas of potential controversy should be phrased only in the broadest terms, using language designed to include as many worthwhile works as possible.

While diverse and "balanced" library collections should be sought, the policy statement should definitely *not* mandate that individual works conform to some standard of objectivity and factual accuracy. In controversial areas, it is often precisely the definition of what can be called "objective" that is at issue. Library collections should include works with distinctive and conflicting points of view on controversial issues, and not only works that purport to stand above the fray and comment evenhandedly on several contesting opinions.

Reconsideration

Despite the quality of the selection process, occasional objections to instructional and library materials are to be expected. Therefore, the procedure for handling complaints and for reconsidering challenged materials should be clearly enunciated in the policy statement. This procedure should establish a framework for registering a complaint that provides for a hearing with appropriate action. At the same time, it should defend the principles of academic freedom, the student's right of access to materials, and the professional responsibility and integrity of the faculty.

Review of challenged materials should be treated objectively and unemotionally—as an important, but routine action. Every effort should be made to weigh objections in the light of established policy criteria. The policy should stress that informal inquiries about curricular matters are welcome, permitting the swift resolution of complaints through calm and courteous discussion.

It must be stressed, however, that informal reviews may only result in the retention of a challenged work. *No materials should be removed without a formal hearing in accordance with the full reconsideration policy.* Moreover, *no materials should be removed upon the authority of a single staff member or school official, up to and including the superintendent of schools.* Removals should be authorized only by a Reconsideration Committee responsible to the school board. Avenues of appeal to the board should be clearly delineated for *both* those who seek a work's removal and those who desire its retention.

The policy should indicate that, if informal discussion does not resolve the issue, a complainant is entitled to file a written complaint. The school district should supply a form for such a complaint, a sample version of which is included in the appendix. The policy should state that the "burden of proof," so to speak, is on those who challenge materials already used in the school. *While the reconsideration process is proceeding, challenged materials should remain available to faculty and students as before.* Although a student whose family has filed an objection to classroom materials may sometimes be temporarily excused from using those materials or given a substitute according to district policy, library resources should remain on open shelves until found—after a full hearing—not to meet selection criteria.

The policy should provide for a Reconsideration Committee. The composition of this committee will vary from place to place according to local conditions. Where possible, it should be a standing and not an ad hoc body, although this may not be possible where challenges are few. Where it is not feasible to indicate the composition of the committee in the policy itself, its method of appointment should be spelled out. Usually, it will be the responsibility of the principal or the district superintendent to name the committee. Direct appointment by the school board or even elective forms of composing the group may also be considered. If nothing else, these methods may protect against the charge that the body has been "packed" to favor a single administrator's desires.

The committee should, in any event, be composed principally of professional staff, including teachers and librarians, with representation from the school administration and, in some smaller districts, perhaps the school board. Many districts also include community members and parents on the Reconsideration Committee. This may be useful in building confidence and trust between the community and the school system, but it should be clearly spelled out that the power to decide the issue rests not with individual parents or activists, but with the responsible professional staff and, ultimately, with the school board, which in most places is elected by the community as a whole. Community members and parents should never constitute a majority on the committee and, if possible, they should have a consultative voice, but no vote. By no means should the person filing the complaint be part of the committee.

Some districts have mandated the inclusion of local clergy on Reconsideration Committees. While religious leaders share with others the right to actively participate as individuals in school affairs and on all school committees, it is not advisable—and probably unconstitutional—for a public school system to *mandate* the participation of local religious authorities in the work of a Reconsideration Committee.

The Reconsideration Committee should have clearly defined procedures for functioning and the policy should indicate to whom its decision is to be referred. Complainants should be given an opportunity to present their specific charges orally, as well as being required to present them in writing. Procedures for organizing public hearings and soliciting testimony in favor of retaining challenged materials should also be spelled out. The Reconsideration Committee should consider all complaints with an open mind and, even if the complainant has not reviewed an entire work, but only "browsed through" it, committee members should still base their judgment on an assessment of the work as a whole. The committee should resolve the controversy by applying the objectives and criteria adopted in the relevant selection policy.

As already noted, avenues of appeal should be open to both those who favor and those who oppose the removal of specific classroom or library materials. Usually, the body to which appeals are addressed will be the school board or, in especially large districts, perhaps a board committee. Procedures for filing appeals with the board should be included in the policy statement. All hearings before the board should be open to the public. Of course, those who do not wish to abide by a board decision have ultimate recourse to the courts, but this will be relatively rare (see chapter 6).

The Completed Policy

It hardly needs to be said that preparation of a complete policy statement requires work—a great amount of it. A model policy is included in the appendix, but no model will be appropriate to each and every district. The final format and organization of the materials selection statement will depend, of course, on the particularities of the school system concerned.

The Completed Policy

One possible table of contents, however, might look like this:

Part 1: Selection of Materials
    I. Statement of Policy
    II. Selection Objectives
    III. Responsibility for Selection
        A. Delegation of Responsibility to Professional Staff
        B. Responsibility for Library/Media Center Selection
        C. Responsibility for Textbook Selection
        D. Responsibility for Selection of Supplementary Classroom Materials
    IV. Selection Criteria
        A. General Criteria
        B. Specific Criteria: Library Materials
        C. Specific Criteria: Classroom Materials
    V. Policy on Controversial Materials
        A. General Statement
        B. *Library Bill of Rights*

Part 2: Selection Procedures
    I. Procedures for Policy Implementation
        A. Selection Aids
        B. Recommendation Procedures
        C. Gifts
        D. Special Concerns
    II. Evaluation and Review of Existing Materials
    III. Procedures for Dealing With Challenges
        A. Request for Informal Review
        B. Request for Formal Review
        C. The Reconsideration Committee
        D. Resolution and Appeal

A Working Document

Once adopted, the materials selection policy should not simply be filed away and forgotten. It must be kept up-to-date and used. All professional staff members should be given a copy of the policy, and workshops should be held to explain its principles and operation.

A good policy can also be an effective organizing tool in defending the district against censorship. The process by which the policy is formulated should provide an opportunity for administrators and staff to familiarize the school board with the important principles upon which a good selection policy will be based. This effort can and should continue once the policy is adopted. It may even be appropriate regularly to resubmit the selection policy statement to review by the board, perhaps after each election. This will provide an opportunity for school officials and staff to "take the pulse" of the board and to express their own continued support for academic and intellectual freedom.

The policy can also be useful in developing public understanding. Some districts have found it effective to print relevant sections of their policy statements as attractive and readable brochures for public distribution. Formulating and maintaining an effective materials selection policy is one way of building a network of support for intellectual freedom in education before a censorship incident occurs. For ultimately the best defense against school censorship is an aroused and supportive community, represented by an informed and committed school board.

Student Rights and the Student Press

In addition to a materials selection statement, school districts need to develop written policies delineating student expressional rights and specifically, where applicable, the rights of student journalists, both those working on periodicals sponsored by the school and those who seek to distribute their own or other outside publications on school grounds.[4]

Such a policy should include a general statement of student rights and responsibilities. Since student expression that will cause "substantial disruption" to school functions may legally be curtailed, the nature of such disruption and examples of impermissible forms of expression should be clearly indicated in language that students will easily understand.

With regard to the student press, according to model guidelines formulated by the Student Press Law Center in Washington, D.C. (see appendix H), a policy statement should:

- Explicitly indicate that school-sponsored publications are "forums for student expression."
- Outline the responsibilities of student journalists.
- List the kinds of materials student publications are prohibited from publishing. These should include *only* obscene, libelous, and "substantially disruptive" material. It should be explicitly indicated that

material stimulating heated discussion or debate does not necessarily constitute the type of disruption prohibited.

- Establish broad guidelines for advertising, if advertising is to be accepted.
- Outline guidelines for the distribution of nonschool-sponsored publications. These publications should enjoy substantially the same protections as sponsored publications.
- Specify the rights of any faculty adviser to a student publication. Ideally, a statement should be included to the effect that no teacher will be disciplined for failure to exercise editorial control over a student publication or to otherwise suppress the rights of free expression of student journalists.

School publications should not be censored because of their treatment of controversial public issues, if that treatment is not libelous, obscene, or an invasion of privacy. School publications policy should not prohibit criticism of school policies or practices, and funds should be guaranteed irrespective of editorial policy. School publications should be allowed to print material written by nonstudents.

What Do We Do If...?

In a democratic society, where it is natural for parents and others to have concern for the education of children, it is reasonable to expect that there will be questions and complaints regarding content of educational resources, class programs, and teaching methods. Such complaints are allowable in our society and should never be labeled as inappropriate or harmful in and of themselves.

Minnesota Civil Liberties Union[1]

When school districts follow the policies and procedures outlined in this book, the overwhelming majority of complaints will be resolved without undue controversy, very often to the mutual satisfaction of the district and the complainant.[2] But sometimes, despite the protections offered by a sound materials selection policy and review procedure, a major censorship incident still develops.

A censorship incident usually begins with a citizen's complaint about specific school library or classroom materials. The complaint may be lodged with the librarian or teacher, or a complainant may go directly to a principal or other administrator or even to a school board member. In general, the complainant's immediate aim is to inform the school that the materials in question are unacceptable, but sometimes there is already an element of "grandstanding" at play.

In some cases, the complainant may assume that the school will immediately agree that the materials are not appropriate. This may reflect ignorance about basic principles of education, which can readily be corrected in one or two informal discussions. In other cases, however, even a neutral response from the school that the complaint will need to be considered according to established review procedures and that until a formal decision is made, the material will remain in use may provoke outrage and charges that the school is harming the community's youth.

A would-be censor may want to state publicly that "objectionable" materials have been found in the schools and may even attend a meeting of the school board to announce this "discovery." Sections of the objectionable work may be read aloud or distributed in writing to the school board, local press, and public, sometimes even before an oral, not to mention written, complaint has been submitted to school personnel.

An ad hoc censorship organization may be formed, or some previously organized pressure group may jump on the censorship bandwagon, sometimes at the initiative of a complainant, but not infrequently without his or her support or even knowledge. Even if a pressure group is loosely organized, would-be censors can use it effectively to promote a statement of purposes among other community groups; to conduct letter-writing campaigns to district officials, board members and the media; and to circulate petitions. The organization might also seek to influence school funding, administrative appointments, and the election of board members.

Some General Rules

When a censorship incident does threaten to mushroom into a crisis, the first basic rule for everyone involved is DO NOT PANIC! No matter how belligerent and seemingly unreasonable complainants or their supporters may become—no matter how much some local politicians, the media, or assorted independent careerists and crusaders may distort the issues—the school district and its professional staff should strive to maintain a calm and professional attitude. Those involved should insist that established policies and procedures be upheld. Though a careful and reasoned response must be made to all allegations, the discussion should be focused on the real issues. Defenders of intellectual and academic freedom should at all times refrain from making personal attacks on their opponents, no matter how justified this may seem at times.

One form of panic is to overreact to a complaint. Although it may be tempting to immediately "pull out all the stops" in meeting a censorship challenge, this could be detrimental. Too many false alarms make it difficult to mobilize broad support when it is truly needed. Outside involvement may also force people and institutions into dogmatic positions from which they find it difficult to compromise or retreat. It is generally not useful to place people in positions in which they will "lose face" by backing down.

Each censorship incident has its own peculiar history. School personnel must generally plot their strategy and tactics on a case-by-case basis. Nevertheless, the following principles have generally proven useful:

- **Keep staff informed.** If the incident involves a single school library or classroom teacher, all professional staff members should be kept fully abreast of the situation as it develops. A lack of internal communication could lead to serious and needless internal controversy and confusion.
- **Keep the board informed.** Make certain that all members of the school district's governing board are kept informed about the incident. Use this opportunity to reinforce their beliefs about the principles of academic freedom.
- **Follow district policy.** Procensorship forces should not be allowed singlehandedly to determine the agenda of debate. As soon as an incident develops, the school district should make clear that censorship is the issue and that existing district selection and review policies offer an adequate defense against truly inappropriate materials. The school's ongoing program of public education about the principles of intellectual freedom should be intensified. All professional staff, board members, media representatives, and concerned citizens should receive a copy of the materials selection policy statement and other relevant materials.
- **Maintain neutrality.** Until a review committee decision is made, the school district should maintain its neutrality about the merits or demerits of the challenged material, both in public statements by review committee members and school officials and by *keeping the material in circulation* pending review. Individual teachers and librarians, however, should be free to defend or criticize any challenged work according to their understanding of its merits and demerits and their interpretation of district policy.
- **Coordinate media relations.** All statements to national, state, and local media should be centrally coordinated. Especially in larger districts where direct communication may be limited, school administrators should be sure to clear all public statements with teachers and librarians directly affected, and vice versa. In dealing with the media, it is important to stress the principles involved in the incident, to point out the implications of censorship for First

Amendment freedoms, and to emphasize the school's responsibility to educate its students to respect the diverse and pluralistic nature of our democracy.

- **Build community support.** Supporters of academic freedom should be informed of all public hearings and board and other meetings where the incident will be discussed. If radio or television talk shows or interviews are scheduled, supporters should be alerted so that they may attend or even participate. Procensorship forces should not be permitted to "stack" the audience at such events.

- **Maintain communication.** In even the most strained situation, lines of communication with the complainants should always remain open. When communication breaks down, debate becomes emotional rather than intellectual. For this reason, it is best to meet with people in small groups, wherever possible. First Amendment rights of teachers and students are not negotiable, but an acceptable and principled solution to a crisis is generally better attained through dialogue than confrontation.

- **Involve legal counsel.** If legal action is threatened, the school district's legal counsel should be so advised at once. If the district does not have legal counsel, assistance can be obtained through several national organizations, including the Freedom to Read Foundation, whose attorneys are also available for consultation with local counsel. Lawsuits that initially seem of only local importance sometimes unexpectedly have a national impact.

- **Thank media, supporters.** When an incident is settled, a responsible representative of the school district should write or personally thank the media representatives, organizations, legislators, officials, and other individuals who came forward to support academic freedom. If the issue is unresolved, these supporters should be kept regularly advised of the situation.

- **Evaluate efforts.** After a challenge is resolved, key members of the professional staff, the school board, relevant government officials, and others involved with the incident should meet to summarize how the issue was handled and consider how procedures might be improved in the future.

Preparing for a Crisis

Well in advance of the appearance of a would-be censor, the school system must establish a materials selection policy, a procedure for handling complaints, and a public relations program. In addition, all

school personnel should be made aware—including through staff training and inservice programs—that at some time there will be complaints about educational materials and resources and, perhaps, about
selection policy as well. As previously noted, school board members
should be kept up-to-date on selection policies and procedures and
they should become familiar with the kinds of materials to be found in
school classrooms and libraries. Both the National Education Association and the American Federation of Teachers have taken strong stands
against school censorship. Administrators may wish to seek ways to
involve local chapters of these teacher organizations in preparing for
censorship incidents.

It is essential to know what attitudes and forces exist in a given
community or state and how these relate to national trends. Which
people in the community have influence? What are their views about
education and intellectual freedom? Which political, social, religious,
business, and labor groups are potential allies? Which are potential
supporters of censorship? What are their principal concerns?

One important source of information and support in opposition to
censorship is the library community. School librarians and administrators should develop a working relationship with the local public library.
They should also be aware that all state library associations maintain
standing Intellectual Freedom Committees that not only provide assistance in times of crisis, but frequently will work with school librarians
to prepare for and prevent incidents. On the national level, the American Library Association maintains a full-time Office for Intellectual
Freedom.

The more that is known about the philosophies and beliefs held by
potential censors, as well as their organizational goals and concerns,
the better prepared schools will be to engage them in meaningful
dialogue. In gathering information on potential censors, however, there
is a danger of opposing censorship with the tactics of the censor.
Educators should avoid practices that involve the prejudgment and
labeling of groups and individuals as censors. Since almost any individual or group with strong opinions can use the tactics of a censor,
maintaining lists of "censorship organizations" and potential complainants is both wrong and ineffective. School personnel should try to
avoid developing an adversary relationship with any individual or
group interested in education, even if that interest seems likely to result
in censorship activity. Building a reputation for receptivity, openness,
fairness, and friendliness toward the *entire* community can only enhance the standing of public schools and strengthen the defense of
academic freedom.

In general, members of the mass media are among the best potential allies in the fight against school censorship. Much has already been done to make the national media aware of the problem. Just about every major television network, every major newspaper, and many national magazines have carried feature stories on challenges to instructional and school library materials. Although the more nationally oriented the media, the more likely they seem to be sympathetic to educators' concerns, many local journalists have proved to be strong supporters of academic freedom.

The media seek out conflict. Hence, at moments of controversy, school administrators, teachers, and librarians may find media attention suddenly thrust upon them. But such attention will be easier to handle, and more likely to result in a fair presentation of the schools' position, if at all times regular contact is maintained with appropriate media personnel. Those charged by a school district with media relations should consider it part of their ongoing activity to publicize the district's materials selection principles and policies. Letters to the editor, newspaper columns, and talk shows are some useful ways to get out the word. In addition, any staff members likely to find themselves at the center of a censorship controversy, should receive some inservice training in public and media relations.

Handling the Initial Complaint

As in handling any type of complaint about school operations, a courteous and calm approach is essential. Above all, complainants must know that they will be given serious consideration and that interest in the schools is welcome. Complainants who come to the school in person or telephone should be listened to courteously and invited to file a written complaint, if the problem cannot be resolved informally. If the complaint comes by letter, it should be acknowledged promptly. In either case, the complainant should be offered a prepared form for submitting a formal challenge. In addition, the rationale for having a formal complaint and review procedure should be explained.

Having a prepared form is not just an additional piece of record-keeping. There are a number of advantages. First, knowing that a response is ready and that there is a procedure to be followed, the teacher, librarian, or administrator will be relieved of much of the initial panic that may arise from a confrontation with an outspoken—even irate—parent or citizen. Also important, the complaint form asks complainants to state their objections in logical, unemotional terms. In addition, the form benefits the complainant. When citizens with com-

Dealing with the News Media

The following general principles will be useful to those contacted by the media:

- Try to get all the information possible about the story or program. Don't be afraid to ask questions of the reporter.
- Have the facts at hand. Avoid commenting without first thinking through the situation. It is permissible to get questions from a reporter and answer them at a later time, especially if the reporter has simply telephoned.
- Don't offer personal opinions. Stick to facts, policy, and the explication of basic principles.
- Try not to become embroiled in particulars. Move the discussion to the larger issue of intellectual freedom and censorship.
- Don't assume those with whom you are speaking know the background of the issue. Be prepared to provide background information and to recommend resources.
- Don't make long speeches. Reduce your arguments to one or two pithy sentences so you won't be quoted "out of context." This is especially important with the broadcast media.
- Control your emotions. Try to identify with your audience and speak to their concerns.
- Try to think of all the questions you might be asked and prepare convincing responses in advance. A meeting with a writer or reporter, or an appearance on radio or television, no matter how brief, needs preparation.

plaints are asked to follow an established procedure for lodging their objections, they feel assured they are being properly heard and that their views will be considered. Filling out the form also compels complainants to "think through" their objections and clearly state their goals.

If the initial complaint is made to a teacher or librarian directly, the appropriate administrator should be immediately informed of the encounter, regardless of its outcome. If the complaint is made to an administrator, one or two members of the professional staff who were involved in the selection decision or who use the material in question should, in most cases, be invited to participate. If the complaint is made to a school board member or to the board as a whole, the complainant should be permitted a brief statement and referred to the appropriate school official. Under no circumstance should a board member respond to such a complaint by voicing an opinion in advance of staff review. Rather, the board should express its confidence in the selection and review policy it has adopted.

In any event, the initial response of the person receiving the complaint should be to *listen*. Find out what concerns motivate the complainant and investigate the complainant's understanding of both the material in question and educational practice. Be sensitive to nonverbal as well as verbal forms of communication. It is not necessary to launch into a thorough defense of the challenged material at this time. Indeed, in some instances it may be advisable to withhold all judgment. More important is to explain how materials are selected and to stress the important principles of academic freedom and respect for diversity and pluralism which form the basis of the selection policy.

The complainant should be informed that the school believes that the overwhelming majority of selection decisions do conform to district criteria, but that a reconsideration procedure is available. Since mistakes are possible, in a few cases the staff member may become convinced that the complaint is clearly justified, that the material in question does not meet district standards. In such a case, this opinion should not be voiced, at that time. The full review procedure should still be followed.

The Reconsideration Committee

As soon as a written complaint form is filed, the objections should be reviewed. The review should consist of specific steps, although the number will vary according to the school situation. Once the committee is appointed, it should do the following:

- First, the person or committee that selected the item or, if not available, an appropriate substitute should evaluate the original reasons for the purchase. The objections should be considered in terms of the school's materials selection policy, broader academic freedom principles, and the opinions of the various reviewing sources used in materials selection.
- Second, the objections and the response should be forwarded to the individual with final responsibility for selection. This may be a teacher, librarian, or administrator, depending upon the school and the nature of the material challenged. Then, this person should prepare a written response to the complaint.

It is critical that the reconsideration process be as objective as possible. The Reconsideration Committee members should all read

any challenged book or periodical, view any challenged film or videotape, or listen to any challenged recording *in its entirety*. The committee
also may consult the publisher of the material about challenges that
might have been filed elsewhere and in order to hear arguments in
defense of the work. Sometimes a publisher will put those involved in
meeting a censorship effort directly in touch with the author of a
challenged work.

Although state open meeting laws vary, it is generally best that the
Reconsideration Committee hold its hearings in public, although requests by individual complainants for anonymity may be respected if
this conforms to state law. It is not necessary to widely publicize a
committee meeting if the complainant has not sought media attention.
The committee should, however, be sure to arrange to hear testimony
from all interested opponents *and* defenders of the challenged material,
including individual teachers, librarians, parents, and citizen activists.

If, as is most often the case, the committee decides that the material does meet the selection criteria and is deemed suitable for continued
use in the schools, the appropriate school official (either the review
committee chair or the administrator who appointed the committee)
should respond promptly to the complaint in writing. This response
should briefly outline the reasoning behind the decision. It should also
inform the complainant how to pursue an appeal and that further
discussion of the decision is welcome. The complainant should be
thanked for his or her interest in the schools.

If They Won't "Play by the Rules"

Although the formal review procedures recommended in this book
ultimately benefit all sides in a censorship conflict, some would-be
censors are, for varying reasons, unwilling to follow accepted public
procedures. Sometimes they will charge that "the deck is stacked"
against them. In other instances, the specific challenge appears less
important than stirring up controversy and staging confrontations for
their own sake, or for the sake of a much broader political or educational agenda.

If a group in the community wants to change the public schools,
that is their right. There is nothing the school district can or should do
to stop them from promoting their cause. However, no objection to
instructional or library materials should be formally considered unless
a written request for reconsideration is filed. This should be an iron-
clad rule. Moreover, the schools cannot stand idly by while would-be

censors work to mold public opinion. A censorship campaign that is not accompanied by a formal challenge should be met with a renewed and vigorous effort by the school district to educate the appropriate authorities and the public about materials selection policies and, most importantly, about the principles of academic and intellectual freedom that underlie them.

Teachers, librarians, parents, and citizens should be free to defend materials that are under attack in the media or elsewhere, all the while making clear that avenues for review remain open. Indeed, censorship campaigns of this sort are often effectively stopped by a forthright challenge to the would-be censors to file a written complaint. If nothing else, this prevents them from continually shifting their rhetoric and demands to prevent a truly constructive resolution of the conflict.

If "The Community Is Up in Arms"

It is always easier to impose one's will if one is perceived to be in the majority. And most would-be censors claim that their views are held by most others. In fact, that is generally not the case. Countless opinion polls and numerous censorship battles have revealed that opponents of curricular and library materials represent a relatively small segment of the public. Few share their objections to specific materials, and even fewer share their willingness to deny access to those materials to others.

This may not always be apparent, however. Through skillful manipulation of petition drives, public rallies, and media attention, would-be censors may appear to command broad support even if their forces are actually quite small. An individual censor may rally others by appearing as a courageous individual up against an entrenched bureaucracy. Those who would defend against censorship, on the other hand, may seem like a true "silent majority." One key to dealing with any censorship campaign is to mobilize the support of this "silent majority" and to give it voice. The goal here is not to "smother" the protest, but to encourage fruitful discussion and debate. In many instances, the more the community is mobilized to really listen to the complainants, the more their support wanes.

Censorship of instructional and school library materials can be resisted by informing a number of support sources. These include:

- Community leaders and community organizations that understand and support the school's defense of academic freedom.
- Local news media.

- Local librarians and other educators in the community and state.
- The publisher of the challenged material and, perhaps, the authors.
- Local, state, and national education and civil liberties groups (see appendix J).

Still, not every censorship effort will be the work of a handful. In some cases, the majority of the community *will* oppose the continued use in class or the school library of some controversial work. Especially in the case of the library, this does not mean that the challenged material needs to be removed or restricted. The sole criterion for such action should be the material's failure to conform to the standards of the district's materials selection policy—assuming these standards themselves conform to the principles of intellectual freedom. In these instances, it is the duty of the schools to uphold the right of the minority against the wishes of the majority. Eighty percent should not deprive twenty percent of their rights. A censorship attempt presents the schools with a good opportunity to explain the philosophy that underlies our system of democratic public education.

If the Challenge Succeeds

It is important to keep in mind that not every attempt to resist censorship will be successful. Some instructional and library materials will be removed or restricted, no matter what policies and procedures are followed and adopted. If the challenged item does not meet a school's own criteria for selection, the school must be ready to acknowledge that it is indeed unsuitable.

A work may be ruled unsuitable by a reconsideration committee because an honest mistake was made in the original selection process. A work may also be ruled unsuitable because the selection policy was not adequate to defend controversial, but educationally suitable, materials. In such a case, teachers, librarians, and administrators should work to revise and improve the selection policy in accordance with the guidelines outlined in this book.

Should a review committee remove or restrict materials that teachers, librarians, administrators, parents, or others believe suitable or in conformity with selection criteria, an appeal can be made to the school board. Should the board reject that appeal or—as more frequently occurs—should it reverse a favorable decision by a reconsideration committee, the anticensorship forces may have to accept what they believe to be an incorrect decision. They may decide that the best course of action is to work more closely with the school board members or to work for their replacement.

There is also the possibility of legal action. The United States Supreme Court has granted local school boards considerable power in the daily operation of school systems. The courts have, however, looked askance at efforts by school boards to impose on students personal biases. Moreover, as discussed at length in the following chapter, in those cases where school boards have violated their own policies, or where these policies clearly contradict constitutional precepts, the courts have ruled in favor of those protesting school board decisions to remove or restrict books, especially from school libraries.

In many instances developments will take a discouraging turn, and each individual will have to decide how forcefully to fight for higher principles and what sacrifices will be acceptable in that fight. It is certain, however, that if educators are not prepared to offer any resistance to censorship pressures, no battle will be won.

6

What Is the Law?

The very purpose of the Bill of Rights was to withdraw certain subjects from the vicissitudes of political controversy, to place them beyond the reach of majorities and officials and to establish them as legal principles to be applied by the courts. One's right to life, liberty and property, to free press, freedom of worship and assembly, and other fundamental rights may not be submitted to vote; they depend on the outcome of no elections.

West Virginia State Board of Education v. Barnette[1]

The 1970s and 1980s probably saw more legal and constitutional challenges to public school library and textbook decisions than in all previous American history. The reasons for this remarkable increase in litigation are no doubt many and varied. As legal scholar Mark Yudof noted:

> Resolution of disputes in the public schools is increasingly dominated by rules and formal procedures and legislation and lawsuits, and it is natural that the legalization apparent with regard to collective bargaining, student records, desegregation, treatment of the handicapped, and the like, should spill over into the textbook area. Public opinion polls also show a declining confidence in professionals and public officials, and many are perhaps less accepting of decisions made by experts or elected school representatives. . . . And with the decline in the view that public schools are above politics, the dissension in values that pervades so many areas . . . may result in an increased willingness of the losers in the political process to do battle in the courts.[2]

The growing body of case law, however, has not reversed the longstanding history of judicial reluctance to become involved in the daily operation of the schools. "The education of the Nation's youth is primarily the responsibility of parents, teachers, and state and local school officials, and not of federal judges," the United States Supreme Court declared in 1988.[3] Still, the courts will get involved in conflicts about education when constitutionally protected rights are violated or when there are questions about the validity of state or federal statutes under the Constitution.

Basic Principles

On the issue of school library and curricular censorship, there is no single definitive judicial opinion, and many critical issues remain unresolved. Nevertheless, three conclusions seem to be substantiated by the diverse judicial record:

- The personal beliefs of individuals—political, social, moral, or religious—*may not* be used to justify the removal of school resources.
- Resources *may* legally be removed for reasons of space, obsolescence, lack of educational suitability, and—here the waters are somewhat murky—perhaps owing to "pervasive vulgarity." The courts, however, do tend to distinguish between the school library and the classroom in determining the limits of school board discretion.
- School board policies and procedures must be followed in all reviews of library and instructional materials. The failure of school boards and their administrative agents to follow constitutionally valid policies and procedures—that is, to abide by due process protections—will, according to the United States Supreme Court, be grounds for invalidating decisions to remove or restrict access to library and instructional materials. Indeed, removals or restrictive decisions that might be permitted by the courts when policies and procedures are followed, are likely to be overturned when these are ignored or violated.

In a nutshell, the message conveyed by outstanding case law appears to be that school personnel would be wise to:

- Use written criteria for the selection of resources.
- Make removal decisions on the basis of the educational suitability of the resource.
- *Not* allow personal views to govern selection or removal decisions.
- Follow appropriate policies and procedures during any review process.

Differing Views and Unresolved Issues

As attorney William North has argued, in most decisions touching upon the rights to intellectual freedom of teachers, librarians, and students, the courts have ruled according to the justices' view of the role of schools in our society. If the school's role is seen primarily as one of indoctrination and inculcation of community values, school boards will have almost unlimited discretion in the selection and removal of materials that are part of the school's curriculum. If, however, the view is that the school is a marketplace of ideas where students may have access to a variety of viewpoints, the limits imposed upon the school board are expanded considerably. Both these views are held to varying degrees by judges at all levels, including the United States Supreme Court. This is hardly surprising given the complexity of the issue, and it is unlikely that the judiciary—even at the highest level—will be able in the foreseeable future to adopt a completely uniform and unambiguous approach.[4]

The legal situation is further complicated not only by disagreements within the judiciary, but also by the continually shifting course of litigation. The most important legal decisions so far have come in cases initiated by those seeking to reverse decisions by local school authorities to remove library or instructional materials. More recently, however, litigants have sought, with little success, to get the courts to remove or somehow restrict the use of materials they find objectionable, usually on the grounds that they violate religious freedoms. In addition, the Supreme Court's 1988 decision in a student press case, *Hazelwood School District* v. *Kuhlmeier*, opened new legal possibilities that the judiciary has only begun to explore.

Most of the cases to date have involved what Robert O'Neil has called "noncirculation decisions" in which school authorities have removed or restricted materials already acquired or used, principally by school libraries or media centers. It is possible, however, to conceive of at least three other situations in which legal reasoning might vary. There is, first, what O'Neil called the "nonacquisition" case, in which an initial judgment *not* to acquire or use some material is challenged by plaintiffs as an act of censorship. Second, moving from the library to the classroom, the courts have begun to examine the "questionable adoption" situation, in which a decision to assign (or to stop assigning) controversial material in class is questioned. Finally, there is the still largely unresolved issue of the "curricular modification" situation, in which a course of study rather than a specified text or other educational resource is challenged or has been modified in a way that might invite legal challenge.[5]

This chapter will not try to predict the possible directions future litigation and legal reasoning may take. Its more modest purpose is to introduce the reader to the historical development and current status of federal law. (Since the issue of intellectual and academic freedom is overwhelmingly a Constitutional question dependent upon judicial interpretation of the First Amendment, virtually all relevant litigation has been carried on in the federal rather than the state courts. Since the *Hazelwood* decision, however, the perception has grown that First Amendment protections of student rights are more limited. In those states whose constitutions provide stronger protections than the First Amendment, litigation involving student expression and school censorship has begun to enter the state courts.)

To be sure, only a small handful of school districts will find themselves embroiled in litigation. Nevertheless, school personnel should have a fundamental awareness of their legal situation. The best defense against a lawsuit is to act according to the law. To do so, it is necessary to know what the law says.

If a real or potential legal problem does arise, school administrators should consult legal counsel. *The information in this book should not be used as a substitute for professional representation and advice.* Few attorneys, however, including many involved in education or working regularly with or for public school systems, are adequately conversant with the myriad subtle issues involved in this area. School districts with regular counsel should encourage their attorneys to become familiar with the issues and cases discussed here *before* a controversy arises.

School Libraries: The *Pico* Decision

"It is easy to forget how recent is the development of law dealing with textbook and curricular censorship," Robert O'Neil wrote in 1983.[6] Before the 1970s, there were a few legal skirmishes, but no case directly addressed the issues with which the courts later became concerned. Then, beginning in 1972, a series of cases began to focus on the question of whether a school board could constitutionally remove from circulation school library books previously acquired and used by students for reasons pertaining to the controversial content of these books.

The issue reached the United States Supreme Court with the case of *Board of Education, Island Trees (New York) Union Free School District 26* v. *Pico*, which was decided on June 25, 1982. Even though it did not produce a majority opinion, the *Pico* case was one of the most significant First Amendment decisions to be rendered by the Supreme Court in the past two decades.

The *Pico* case involved the right of one junior high school and four high school students to challenge the removal from school libraries by a Long Island school board of all copies of nine books because they were, in the board's view, "anti-American, anti-Christian, anti-Semitic, and just plain filthy." Five books were removed despite a committee report that recommended their retention. There was evidence, too, that the board violated its own policies and procedures.

The District Court granted summary judgment in favor of the board but, on appeal, a three-judge panel of the United States Court of Appeal for the Second Circuit by a 2–1 majority reversed that decision, remanding the case for trial. The Supreme Court upheld that reversal by a narrow 5–4 margin. Rather than go to trial, the school board returned the books to the shelves and reached an out-of-court settlement.

"Just as access to ideas makes it possible for citizens generally to exercise their rights of free speech and press in a meaningful manner, such access prepares students for active and effective participation in the pluralistic, often contentious society in which they will soon be adult members," Justice William J. Brennan, Jr., wrote in the lead opinion.

According to Brennan's opinion in *Pico*, school boards have:

> significant discretion to determine the content of their school libraries. But that discretion may not be exercised in a narrowly partisan or political manner. . . . If petitioners [the school board] *intended* by their removal decision to deny respondents access to ideas with which petitioners disagreed, and if this intent was the decisive factor in petitioners' decision, then petitioners have exercised their discretion in violation of the Constitution.[7]

The Court noted that the Island Trees school board's failure to follow established procedures lent support to suspicions about its motives. "This would be a very different case if the record demonstrated that petitioners had employed established, regular, and facially unbiased procedures for the review of controversial materials," Brennan wrote.

Only three other justices joined Brennan's plurality opinion, however. Moreover, Brennan emphasized "the limited nature of the substantive question presented by the case," which applied only to "*library* books, books that by their nature are optional rather than required books" and did "not involve the *acquisition* of books." The court identified, without definition or explanation, "pervasive vulgarity" and "educational suitability" as constitutionally valid reasons for removal of school library books. This lack of definition also limits application of the decision to subsequent cases.

The Lower Courts: An Ambiguous Record

Pico did not resolve all the issues raised by previous lower court and appellate decisions and these must still be considered an important part of outstanding case law.[8] The earliest school library book suppression opinion was the United States Court of Appeals for the Second Circuit's 1972 decision in *Presidents Council, District 25 v. Community School Board No. 25* (New York City). There, the court upheld the removal of a library book on the ground that court action against the board was precluded by the Supreme Court's evolution decision in *Epperson v. Arkansas*. In *Presidents Council*, the court did not perceive the elimination of the book as involving an effort to aid or oppose religion, nor did it perceive the elimination of the book from the library as analogous to a ban on nondisruptive silent speech, which the Supreme Court condemned in *Tinker v. Des Moines Independent School District*.[9]

In 1976, the Court of Appeals for the Sixth Circuit was confronted, in *Minarcini v. Strongsville (Ohio) City School District*, with a challenge to the removal of Joseph Heller's *Catch 22* and two novels by Kurt Vonnegut. In contrast to the Second Circuit, the court in *Minarcini* held that "[t]he removal of books from a school library is a much more serious burden upon freedom of classroom discussion than the action found unconstitutional in *Tinker*...." It based this holding, first, on its perception that "[a] library is a mighty resource in the free marketplace of ideas" and, second, on its understanding that the First Amendment protects the "right to know."[10]

Relying on *Minarcini*, in 1978, a Massachusetts district court required a school board to return to the high school library an anthology that included a poem the committee found "objectionable," "obnoxious," "filthy," and "vile and offensive garbage." (*Right to Read Defense Committee v. School Committee of the City of Chelsea*.) The court found that "no substantial governmental interest was served by" removing the book. As in *Minarcini*, the Court distinguished between the school board's power to control curriculum content and its power to control library collections. It also distinguished between the school board's power to select books for the library and its power to remove books, once selected. Adopting the *Chelsea* analysis, in 1979, the Federal District Court for New Hampshire, in *Salvail v. Nashua Board of Education*, required the board to return to its high school library copies of *Ms.* magazine because the school district had failed "to demonstrate a substantial and legitimate government interest sufficient to warrant the removal...."[11]

The 1980s opened with two federal circuits presented with three major cases challenging the removal of materials from high school libraries. In two of these cases, the challenge was rejected. The third case was *Pico*.

In *Zykan v. Warsaw (Indiana) Community School Corporation*, which came before the Seventh Circuit Court, the record showed that the school board had turned "offending" books over to complaining citizens who caused them to be burned. While the court condemned this ceremony, it still concluded that the complaint failed to state a cause of action. The court held that:

> ...two factors tend to limit the relevance of "academic freedom" at the secondary school level. First, the student's right to and need for such freedom is bounded by the level of his or her intellectual development. ...Second, the importance of secondary schools in the development of intellectual faculties is only one part of a broad formative role encompassing the encouragement and nurturing of those fundamental social, political, and moral values that will permit a student to take his place in the community.... [Therefore,] complaints filed by secondary school students to contest the educational decisions of local authorities are sometimes cognizable but generally must cross a relatively high threshold before entering upon the field of a constitutional claim suitable for federal court litigation.[12]

While the Seventh Circuit was deciding *Zykan*, the Second Circuit was presented with two opportunities to reconsider its 1972 *Presidents Council* opinion. The first was *Pico* and the second was *Bicknell v. Vergennes Union High School Board of Directors*. Decided the same day, by the same panel, both *Pico* and *Bicknell* involved the removal from school libraries of books of considerable literary reputation. The dismissal of the complaint in *Bicknell* was affirmed and the dismissal of the complaint in *Pico* was reversed, both by 2–1 majorities. One judge saw both cases as an unconstitutional effort to purge the school library of ideas deemed inconsistent with the value inculcation objectives of the curriculum. A second judge saw both cases as an appropriate and constitutionally proper exercise of the value inculcation function. The deciding judge in each case distinguished between *Bicknell* and *Pico* on the basis of the board's motive for removal. In *Bicknell*, he found the motive to be the books' "vulgar and indecent language," which justified removal, while in *Pico*, he found the motive to be the books' "ideas" or content, apart from vulgar or indecent language, which did not justify removal.[13]

As William North has commented:

> While all of these cases, including *Pico*, arose in the context of First Amendment challenges to the removal of books from school libraries, they all turned on differences in judicial perceptions of the proper role of school officials in the educational process. As a consequence, the primary effect of the Supreme Court's consideration in *Pico* was to identify what must be characterized as a fundamental philosophical dispute over the nature and function of elementary and secondary education in America. This dispute, revealed most graphically in the *Pico* opinions, has divided the Court into two substantially equal and determined factions.[14]

In fact, the "factional" division extends throughout the judicial system, which should come as little surprise. The courts are no more immune from our national debate over education than any other institution. Moreover, the debate is a continuous one which, perhaps, can never be brought to a close. As a result, school administrators, faculty, and librarians should expect the law governing school and school library censorship cases to continue to evolve.

Religion in the Schools

Since *Pico*, the focus of litigation has shifted from the library to the classroom. Cases decided over the last decade have mainly involved appeals to

---

History Tells Us . . .

In a nutshell, the message conveyed by outstanding case law appears to be that school personnel would be wise to:

- Use written criteria for the selection of resources.
- Make removal decisions on the basis of the educational suitability of the resource.
- *Not* allow personal views to govern selection or removal decisions.
- Follow appropriate policies and procedures during any review process.

the courts by opponents of controversial materials to eliminate or exempt their children from classroom instruction or instructional materials they find objectionable on religious grounds. Other such lawsuits have contested materials as a violation of the First Amendment's ban on the establishment by government of a religious orthodoxy that is somehow secular in nature.

The most celebrated cases have been that of the Church Hill, Tennessee, parents who sought exemption for their children from a reading program that allegedly inculcated values at odds with their fundamentalist religion (*Mozert* v. *Hawkins County*), which was discussed in chapter 2; and the Mobile, Alabama, case (*Smith* v. *Board of School Commissioners*) which led to the temporary court-ordered removal of 44 "secular humanist" textbooks from the state's public schools (see chapter 3). Both decisions were reversed on appeal. The Supreme Court refused to consider a further appeal in *Mozert*, and the *Smith* plaintiffs declined to seek Supreme Court review. More recently, legal challenges to the *Impressions* reading series and some other works charging that adoption of these works amounted to the establishment of occult or "New Age" religion have been rejected by United States District Courts in California, Illinois, and Pennsylvania (see chapter 3).[15]

These cases and the legal controversy over the teaching of Darwinian evolution have focused considerable attention on the legal parameters defining the relationship between religious belief and public education. It is beyond the scope of this book to give guidance to school administrators and personnel on their legal rights and responsibilities with respect to religion in the schools. The American Association of School Administrators in 1986 published a pamphlet on *Religion in the Public Schools*, which provides an exhaustive yet accessible treatment of all the major legal issues.[16] Here it is necessary only to summarize briefly a few legal principles and decisions of special relevance to the censorship issue and to discuss at somewhat greater length the Supreme Court's 1987 decision in *Edwards* v. *Aguillard*, which declared unconstitutional a Louisiana statute mandating the teaching of "creation science" whenever evolution is taught.

The First Amendment's guarantee of religious liberty contains two clauses, commonly referred to as the "Establishment Clause" and the "Free Exercise Clause": "Congress shall make no law respecting an *establishment* of religion, or prohibiting the *free exercise* thereof." Scholars and judges have engaged in extensive debate over what the authors of the Bill of Rights intended by these two clauses. As Supreme Court Justice Sandra Day O'Connor observed, however:

> The simple truth is that free public education was virtually nonexistent in the late eighteenth century. . . . Since there then existed few government-run schools, it is unlikely that the persons who drafted the First Amendment, or the state legislators who ratified it, anticipated the problems of interaction of church and state in the public schools.[17]

The Supreme Court itself has noted that, "It is far easier to agree on the purpose that underlies the First Amendment's Establishment and Free Exercise Clauses than to obtain agreement on the standards that should govern their application."[18] Nonetheless, some general standards have developed. With respect to the Free Exercise Clause, Supreme Court opinions lead to the conclusion that a religious practice is protected if it can pass three tests:

- It must be dictated directly by religious beliefs that are sincerely held.
- It must not seriously interfere with a compelling or overriding state interest.
- The state interest may be achieved by an alternative method that does not restrict the religious practice.[19]

Interpretation of the Establishment Clause has most frequently been at issue in recent school censorship litigation. As Justice Brennan wrote in 1987, "The Court has been particularly vigilant in monitoring compliance with the Establishment Clause in elementary and secondary schools. . . . Consequently, the Court has been required often to invalidate statutes which advance religion in public elementary and secondary schools."[20]

The classic enumeration of the limitations on government mandated by the Establishment Clause was written by Justice Hugo Black in 1947:

> Neither a state nor the Federal Government can set up a church. Neither can pass laws which aid one religion over another. Neither can force nor influence a person to go or to remain away from church against his will or force him to profess a belief or disbelief in any religion. No person can be punished for entertaining or professing religious beliefs or disbeliefs, for church attendance or non-attendance. No tax in any amount . . . can be levied to support any religious activities or institutions, whatever they may be called, or whatever form they may adopt to teach or practice religion. Neither a state nor the Federal Government can, openly or secretly, participate in the affairs of any religious organizations or groups and vice versa.[21]

In 1971, in the case of *Lemon* v. *Kurtzman*, the Supreme Court devised a three-pronged test to determine whether legislation comports with the Establishment Clause. To be constitutionally permissible under the "*Lemon* test," a statute or practice must:

- Have been adopted with a secular purpose.
- Have a principal or primary effect that neither advances nor inhibits religion.
- Not result in an "excessive entanglement of government with religion."[22]

State action violates the Establishment Clause if it fails to satisfy any of the three prongs of the *Lemon* test.

Applying these various principles, the courts have found constitutional violations in school-sponsored prayer or devotional Bible readings, strictly limited public aid to religious schools, and struck down a variety of statutes and practices that sought to introduce religious instruction in the public schools, while continuing to recognize the schools' freedom to teach *about* religion.

By the late 1980s, however, a majority of the Supreme Court had expressed unhappiness with the *Lemon* test and many observers anticipated that the case of *Lee* v. *Weisman*, in which a Jewish family challenged an officially sponsored non-denominational prayer included in the program of a public school graduation, might provide an opportunity for the justices to abandon or radically revise the test. Instead, however, led by Justice Anthony Kennedy, the Court by a 5–4 margin barred the prayer and upheld the test, at least in the school context.

"The First Amendment's religion clauses mean that religious beliefs and religious expression are too precious to be either proscribed or prescribed by the state," Kennedy wrote. If citizens are "subjected to state-sponsored religious exercises," the government itself fails in its "duty to guard and respect that sphere of inviolable conscience and belief which is the mark of a free people. . . . No holding by this Court suggests that a school can persuade or compel a student to participate in a religious exercise."[23]

Evolution and Creation

The issue of religion in the curriculum has been most focused perhaps in the debate over the teaching of evolution and "creationism," which is also clearly joined to the censorship/selection controversy. As previously noted, in 1968, the Supreme Court ruled in *Epperson* v. *Arkansas* that a ban on the teaching of evolution is constitutionally impermissible. "There is and can be no doubt that the First Amendment does not permit the State to require that teaching and learning must be tailored to the principles or prohibitions of any religious sect or dogma," Justice Abe Fortas wrote for the Court.[24]

In other words, the Court held that it is unconstitutional for school districts to remove a particular subject—or, by implication, a specified educational resource or instructional material—from the curriculum primarily *to accommodate the religious views of a particular group of citizens*, even where that group may be the majority. But the Court also implied that school officials have other grounds for removing subject matter. In a concurring opinion, Justice Black wrote: "[T]here is no reason . . . why a State is without power to withdraw from its curriculum any subject deemed too emotional and controversial for its public schools."[25] In most cases, the Court reaffirmed, control of educational policy should be left to state and local authorities.

Epperson covered only the question of *excluding* certain material from the curriculum primarily on religious grounds. However, in 1987, the Supreme Court ruled unconstitutional a Louisiana statute requiring public schools that teach the theory of evolution to *include* in their course of study "creation science" as well. The 7–2 decision in *Edwards* v. *Aguillard* said the state's "balanced treatment" law, enacted in 1981 but never enforced, lacked a clear secular purpose and violated the constitutionally required separation of church and state. The decision did not bar the teaching of creation science, but said a legislature could not require it.

"The Louisiana Creationism Act advances a religious doctrine by requiring either the banishment of the theory of evolution from public school classrooms or the presentation of a religious viewpoint that rejects evolution in its entirety," Justice William J. Brennan, Jr., wrote for the majority. "The act violates the Establishment Clause . . . because it seeks to employ the symbolic and financial support of government to achieve a religious purpose."[26]

Although the Louisiana law contained no references to God, a Creator, the Bible, or any religion, Brennan declared that it was enacted in the context of the historic collisions between religious movements and scientific advocates of evolutionary theory. "The purpose of the Creationism Act was to restructure the science curriculum to conform with a particular religious viewpoint," he wrote. "Out of the many possible science subjects taught in the public schools, the legislature chose to affect the teaching of the one scientific theory that historically has been opposed by certain religious sects."[27]

Student Rights and Student Press

In 1969, the U.S. Supreme Court first explicitly recognized that public school students enjoy First Amendment protections. In *Tinker* v. *Des*

Moines Independent Community School District, the Court made the oft-quoted statement, "It can hardly be argued that either students or teachers shed their rights to freedom of speech or expression at the schoolhouse gate."[28] Although *Tinker* involved the issue of symbolic expression (wearing black armbands), other federal and state courts subsequently applied its principles to cases involving direct student speech and student publications. These cases have given students important rights to free expression and to a free student press.

It is outside the scope of this book to offer a full discussion of the law governing student press rights and responsibilities, although this issue has become increasingly controversial and important in many schools and colleges. The Washington-based Student Press Law Center in 1985 published a detailed and informative study, *Law of the Student Press*, which is recommended to school administrators seeking clarity on this topic.[29] The paragraphs that follow briefly summarize the most general points.

The argument is frequently made that, as "publishers," school officials have complete control over the material that appears in their official school publications. The fact that a school may make a school newspaper an "official" publication and contribute heavily to its financing, however, does not necessarily give school officials full control over the material that appears in the publication. According to the Supreme Court's 1988 landmark student press decision in *Hazelwood School District* v. *Kuhlmeier*, it is crucial to determine if school authorities "by policy or by practice" have intentionally made the publication an open forum for student expression. When that is the case, school-sponsored publications enjoy much of the press rights guaranteed to outside newspapers. If the publication is reserved for another purpose, however, and no public forum has been created, then "school officials may impose reasonable restrictions on the speech of students, teachers, and other members of the school community."[30]

The reasoning in *Hazelwood* implies a distinction, still vaguely defined, between "official" publications produced as part of the classroom curriculum and those for which students do not receive any sort of academic credit. Even when a student publication does not qualify as a public forum the school cannot always dictate that publication's content. As one lower court succinctly put it, "The state is not necessarily the unrestrained master of what it creates and fosters."[31]

The *Hazelwood* decision was in dramatic contrast to the decisions of courts across the country that had, over the previous two decades given student journalists extensive First Amendment protections. Writing for the Supreme Court in *Hazelwood*, Justice Byron White set out the school's authority over the expressive activities that it sponsors:

Educators are entitled to exercise greater control over [school-sponsored] student expression to assure that participants learn whatever lessons the activity is designed to teach, that readers or listeners are not exposed to material that may be inappropriate for their level of maturity, and that the views of the individual speaker are not erroneously attributed to the school. Hence, a school may in its capacity as publisher of a school newspaper or producer of a school play "disassociate itself" ... not only from speech that would "substantially interfere with [its] work ... or impinge upon the rights of other students," ... but also from speech that is, for example, ungrammatical, poorly written, inadequately researched, biased or prejudiced, vulgar or profane, or unsuitable for immature audiences.[32]

In short, the Court declared, when a school's decision to censor a student publication (or other form of student expression) that is not a public forum for student expression is "reasonably related to legitimate pedagogical concerns" it will be permissible. "It is only when the decision to censor a school-sponsored publication, theatrical production, or other vehicle of student expression has no valid educational purpose that the First Amendment is so 'directly and sharply implicate[d],' as to require judicial intervention to protect students' constitutional rights."[33]

The *Hazelwood* decision was also particularly mindful of the school's responsibility for any libelous statements in one of its publications, as well as the effect of an invasion of privacy on a student or the student's family in the closed community of a school. For these reasons, the decision said that "[a] school need not tolerate student speech that is inconsistent with its 'basic educational mission,' ... even though the government could not censor similar speech outside the school."[34]

The majority's opinion drew a sharp dissent from Justice William J. Brennan, Jr., joined by Justices Thurgood Marshall and Harry Blackmun, who declared that the First Amendment prohibits "censorship of any student expression that neither disrupts classwork nor invades the rights of others, and ... any censorship that is not narrowly tailored to serve its purpose."[35]

The long-term impact of *Hazelwood* on student journalism remains unclear five years after the decision, although controversies over student press censorship have certainly mushroomed. In California, the nation's largest state, Section 48907 of the Education Code forbids school officials from censoring student journalism unless a story is "obscene, libelous, slanderous," or advocates "substantial disruption" of the school system. According to the California code, even where censorship is permitted, school officials carry the burden of "showing justification, without undue delay, prior to any limitation of student expression." In the wake of the Supreme Court decision similar provisions have been adopted by some other states and have been proposed in quite a few more. Although *Hazelwood* enhanced the power that school officials may wield over student expression, it by no means advocated the exercise of that power in all or even most permissible instances. Whatever the ultimate effects of the ruling may be, the school's obligation to promote respect for and understanding of free press principles remains unchallenged.

The courts have also several times found that unofficial or so-called "underground" student publications are protected by the First Amendment and that they enjoy the right to distribution on school grounds. After *Hazelwood*—which distinguished between officially sponsored materials and "personal statements"—these protections remain. Indeed, it is not entirely clear whether students legally denied the right to publish material in an official, curricular publication may not, in certain cases, be free to circulate the same material in an "underground" fashion. The courts have recognized, however, that school officials may make reasonable regulations at least as to the time, place, and manner of distribution of unofficial publications.[36]

In fact, school officials may find that the distinction drawn by the Supreme Court between censorship of school-sponsored or curricular publications and "personal statements" may not be so easy to define or enforce and, legal considerations aside, it may even, at times, cause administrators more trouble than it prevents. In December 1987, for example, an Arlington, Virginia, principal decided to ban a student survey on drug and alcohol use from a high school yearbook. According to *Hazelwood* this act of censorship may well have been legal. However, in response some students began organizing a clearly unofficial and extracurricular group they called "Free Press," which sought to distribute pamphlets, armbands, and stickers on school grounds. According to both *Tinker* and *Hazelwood*, legally the principal could not do much to restrict this protest activity.[37]

Although *Tinker* indicated that students are entitled to strong First Amendment protection, it did not give them rights coextensive with those of adults. Because of the peculiar characteristics of the school environment, the Court declared that it would allow school officials to restrict student expression only when it "materially disrupts classwork or involves substantial disorder or invasion of the rights of others."[38] Subsequent lower court decisions have developed and applied this standard in determining when censorship of student publications is permissible.

The *Tinker* ruling made clear that "substantial disruption" requires more than "the discomfort and unpleasantness that always accompany an unpopular viewpoint."[39] Although actual disruptions need not occur to justify censorious action, the burden is on the school to show that its fears of disruption are well-founded. In most instances, courts have required evidence of a potential *physical* disruption of school functioning.

Most courts have recognized that material that is obscene as to minors can be censored. To be legally obscene, though, even for minors, something must be sexually explicit and appeal to a prurient interest, not just be profane or offensive. Several court decisions have found that "earthy words relating to bodily functions and sexual intercourse" may not be censored from student newspapers.[40] However, the freedom to publish that kind of material may be limited by the age of the students to whom the publication is distributed.

The Supreme Court's 1986 decision in *Bethel School District No. 403 v. Fraser*, decided by a 7–2 margin, suggested that "vulgar and offensive" terms and "offensively lewd and indecent" forms of speech, though permissible to adults, may also lie beyond the constitutional protections afforded students. *Fraser* upheld the punishment of a student who used sexual puns in a speech before a school assembly and thus involved a verbal intrusion on students who were, in effect, a captive audience. Whether the Supreme Court will apply *Fraser* to student publications remains unclear. Justice Brennan's concurring opinion in the case specifically stated that he, for one, would not do so, though the *Hazelwood* majority suggested, in a footnote, that they would.

The courts have also concluded that libelous material may be censored from student publications by high school officials. However, there appear to be no reported cases in which a high school publication lost a libel suit, and school officials seeking to exercise censorship on these grounds must proceed with great care and caution. The Supreme Court has declared that statements of pure opinion usually expressed in the form of an editorial cannot be libelous. Hence, an editorial complaining that a principal's policy permitting paddling of students by teachers was the "product of a sick mind" was ruled an expression of opinion, which would not have been the case had the paper untruthfully claimed that the principal had spent time in a mental hospital.[41]

Moreover, public figures alleging libel face a more difficult task in proving the charge than do other plaintiffs. Not only must the allegation be false, but it must be shown to have been motivated by actual malice or a reckless disregard of the facts. There is no easy formula to determine who is or is not a public figure, but several cases suggest that in most situations, statements about a school official relating to the performance of his or her duties will be considered as if the official were a public figure.[42]

Library and Curricular Censorship after *Hazelwood*

Many critics fear that the *Hazelwood* decision could become a rogue elephant upsetting the entire field of established First Amendment precedents because it appears to place educationally motivated censorship beyond the ambit of First Amendment protections.[43] *Hazelwood*, it is argued, could render much of the judicial record reviewed in the earlier sections of this chapter largely irrelevant. To date, however, there is little in the judicial record to suggest anything close to such a sweeping reversal. After all, even in *Tinker* and *Pico*, the Supreme Court recognized that legitimate educational purposes can justify some infringement of free expression.

Still, one relatively new pattern is discernable. The most plausible "educational reason," in the eyes of the courts, for removing a book is because it is vulgar or indecent. Vulgarity and indecency, of course, are not constitutionally acceptable reasons for banning material from, say, a public library. But, courts have found on the basis of *Hazelwood*, that "the special characteristics of the school environment" make these permissible criteria.

Applying the Supreme Court's arguments in *Hazelwood*, the United States Court of Appeals for the Eleventh Circuit in 1989 upheld a Florida school board's removal of a previously approved classroom text because of its perceived vulgarity and sexual explicitness. In *Virgil v. School Board of Columbia County*, a high school literature textbook was banned because of selections from *Lysistrata*, the classic Greek comedy by Aristophanes, and *The Miller's Tale*, by Geoffrey Chaucer. The court was compelled to "seriously question how young persons just below the age of majority can be harmed by these masterpieces of Western literature," but still upheld the school board's censorship action.

The court focused on two aspects of the case. First, was the curricular nature of the material which seemed to give the material in question the imprimatur of school approval. Second, was the argument that the book was removed for "explicit sexuality and excessively vulgar language," which was held to be a legitimate pedagogical concern, although in previous cases the same circuit disallowed censorship of violent materials and materials that allegedly threatened religious and family values as "ideologically motivated."[44]

The court found the school board's action reasonable because the textbook, as well as other versions of the disputed selections, remained in the school library. A similar differentiation between curricular activity and other activities within the school environment was adopted by a federal court in New York in 1989 in the case of *Romano* v. *Harrington*, where a faculty advisor's responsibility for supervising the content of an extracurricular student newspaper was at issue.[45] These cases, building on *Hazelwood*, appear to establish even more firmly the distinction between library and classroom materials.

7

School System Checklist

Selection and review procedures can help when school materials are challenged; but there is no substitute for good community relations in reducing those challenges in the first place.

Michelle Marder Kamhi.[1]

The following checklist of suggestions summarizes the principal actions school districts should take to prepare for and respond to censorship efforts.

Preparation

Before challenges arise, school districts should:

Adopt a written materials selection policy. Policy statements should specify the criteria and procedures for selecting curricula and library materials. The policy should conform to all applicable federal and state laws and to relevant court rulings (see chapter 6). It should endorse the American Library Association's Library Bill of Rights and the principles of intellectual and academic freedom in general. School personnel, including administrators at all levels, should be familiar with and strictly adhere to the established policy and procedures in the selection of all material. The policy should be approved and regularly reviewed by the school board.

Establish, in writing, a clearly defined procedure for dealing with complaints. Formal procedures for the review of challenged materials should be integral to the selection policy statement. Review procedures should, *inter alia*, include:

- A "request-for-review" form to be used to identify, in writing, the complainant's specific concerns and objections, for evaluation during the review process.
- A broad-based committee to review challenged materials. The committee may include parents and community leaders as well as teachers, librarians, and school administrators, but it should be structured so that the review decision will be made according to professional application of written policies.
- A provision barring any restrictions on the use of challenged materials until the entire review process has been completed.
- Avenues for appeal of review committee decisions by both those who oppose and those who favor continued use of the challenged material.

Maintain communication between school personnel and the school board. School administrators have the responsibility to keep board members well-informed about selection policies and practices. It is especially important that the board be made aware of any and all pressures exerted on the schools by outsiders to restrict materials or alter teaching practices.

Establish and maintain continuing communication with the public served by the schools. School personnel should keep the local community informed, on a regular basis, about educational objectives, curricula, and classroom and library programs, and should be accessible to all concerned local residents to hear their views. It is especially important that the community be informed about the policies and procedures for selecting and reviewing books and other instructional and library materials.

Seek to work with all groups and individuals in the community who support intellectual freedom and oppose censorship. As part of their public relations activities, school districts should work with the local media, parent and citizen groups, and professional organizations to develop programs and resources aimed at enlightening the public about the censorship problem and about the principles of academic freedom.

Response

If a challenge arises, school districts should:

Treat all complainants with courtesy and respect. There should be no such thing as a groundless complaint. Those who complain about educational resources vary widely in their life experience, educational level attained, sophistication, and in the nature of their commitment to democratic public education. Virtually all, however, hold sincere and deeply rooted convictions, which school personnel are bound to respect. Even where complainants resort to abusive language or behavior, school personnel should strive at all times to maintain a professional and dignified demeanor with both protesters and the general public.

Attempt to resolve the challenge informally. When a complaint is first received, appropriate personnel should meet informally with the complainant to hear the specific objections being raised and to explain how and why the challenged material was selected. If at the end of this informal discussion, the complainant still wishes to challenge the material in question, the request-for-review form should be provided. *No material should be removed or restricted without a formal review of a written complaint according to procedures outlined in the materials selection policy.* This should be the case even when individual school personnel who meet with a complainant conclude that a mistake has indeed been made in selection and that the complaint is justified.

Act promptly to review challenged materials when a formal request has been filed. When a written request for review is submitted, established review procedures should be implemented immediately and according to school policy. At this time, the school board or other governing body should be fully informed of the details of the complaint. If there is no standing review committee, the necessary committee should now be established.

Strictly adhere to established procedures throughout the review process. All school personnel should be reminded that no restrictions are to be placed on the use of the challenged material until the entire review process has been completed. Individual teachers and librarians should be free to defend or criticize challenged materials, but until a decision has been made, members of the review committee, administrators, and the district as a whole should take a neutral stance. Complaints made by individual school personnel or by school board members should be treated exactly as a complaint submitted by a parent or community member. In no instance should a decision to remove or restrict library or instructional materials be made by a single individual. Failure to follow school policies and procedures and to provide due process protections may leave the school liable to legal action.

Inform the general public. Any review of challenged materials should be conducted openly. However, when a complainant seeks anonymity and does not attempt to exploit the incident in the media, the school district should act accordingly. On the other hand, if public attention is drawn to an incident, the district should work vigorously to keep the community informed through the media and local organizational channels, such as the parents' association or school newsletters. Attention should be focused on the issue of censorship and academic freedom and on the district's selection policy and, to a lesser degree, on the challenged material itself. School personnel should avoid personal attacks on complainants or their supporters and should respond to any attacks on themselves of that sort in a professional and dignified manner.

Seek support. Although very few challenges will end up in court, it is wise to consult legal counsel early in the review process. In addition, local and national groups can offer advice and support. It is best to alert such groups when a complaint is first received. They can often help schools resolve challenges equitably; at the very least, they can provide moral support and resources. (A list of national organizations that offer information and, in some cases, legal advice or other assistance to those involved in censorship disputes is included as appendix J.)

8

Conclusion

The vigilant protection of constitutional freedoms is nowhere more vital than in the community of American schools.

Shelton v. Tucker[1]

If freedom of expression becomes merely an empty slogan in the minds of enough children, it will be dead by the time they are adults.

Nat Hentoff, *The First Freedom*[2]

The policies and procedures recommended in this book may help ensure that conflicts over instructional and library materials will be resolved more equitably, with less damage to academic freedom. But the conflicts themselves demand precious time and energy, and their occurrence can signal the existence of deeper problems. To be sure, many of these problems are societal, beyond the control of educators. But very often, to paraphrase a famous movie line, what we have here is a failure of communication.

If there is a single lesson to be learned from the past two decades of controversy over education, it is that more and better communication is needed. Parents and citizens need to hear more from educators; and educators need to listen more carefully to their critics in the public. Nearly 15 years ago June Berkley, a veteran of 21 years of teaching high school English in a small Ohio town, wrote:

> Discontent with printed material does not always come directly from the book itself; but rather . . . reflects some other dissatisfaction with the school—or the teacher or the system in general. . . . Somehow the school, the teachers themselves, must reestablish confidence in their service to the community. They must make their good efforts understood.[3]

Berkley wrote from experience. A few years earlier, some parents at her school began circulating rumors about a "dirty book" assigned to their children: Robert Newton Peck's *A Day No Pigs Would Die*. In response, the English Department—under Berkley's leadership—set up a special evening course for parents. The course, to which teachers donated their own time, was entitled "Books Our Children Read."

Like many who challenge library and instructional materials, the Ohio parents who were circulating the rumors had not read Peck's book. But now, for their weekly classes, parents were reading this book and others like it, and discussing the books with their children's teachers. The teachers, many of whom were young and as yet without children of their own, learned a few things from the parents about how the children might respond. And the parents learned to love the books and to trust and respect the teachers.

When informed about the censorship threat, too many educators respond defensively, fearful of those who would confront them. In doing so, however, they may merely be mirroring the fears of the censors themselves. According to Dorothy M. Broderick, many would-be censors are people "who find themselves living in a hostile world, surrounded by enemies 'out to get them.' They are people whose world is filled with 'oughts' and 'shoulds' and any indication that other people are freer in their decision-making processes arouses in them severe feelings of anxiety and resentment."[4]

If this is true, then it is imperative that public schools reach out to these people *before* controversy arises. The issue of school censorship is not an issue only for teachers, librarians, and school administrators. It is not only a concern for parents. Public education is crucial to the future of our society. And freedom in the public schools is central to the quality of what and how students learn.

Indeed, the proper functioning of our free society demands that the public schools bring together youth of all classes and origins and provide them with instruction that will allow them to participate fully in democratic life. In the words of philosopher Sidney Hook, such instruction "encourages, commensurate with the intellectual powers of students, questioning as integral to learning."[5] To accomplish this purpose requires more freedom, not less, in the classroom and the school library.

Access to Resources and Services in the School Library Media Program

An Interpretation of the Library Bill of Rights

The following is an interpretation of the Library Bill of Rights as it relates to access to library and media resources and services. It was adopted by the ALA Council in 1986 and amended in 1990.

The school library media program plays a unique role in promoting intellectual freedom. It serves as a point of voluntary access to information and ideas and as a learning laboratory for students as they acquire critical thinking and problem solving skills needed in a pluralistic society. Although the educational level and program of the school necessarily shapes the resources and services of a school library media program, the principles of the Library Bill of Rights apply equally to all libraries, including school library media programs.

School library media professionals assume a leadership role in promoting the principles of intellectual freedom within the school by providing resources and services that create and sustain an atmosphere of free inquiry. School library media professionals work closely with teachers to integrate instructional activities in classroom units designed to equip students to locate, evaluate, and use a broad range of ideas effectively. Through resources, programming, and educational processes, students and teachers experience the free and robust debate characteristic of a democratic society.

School library media professionals cooperate with other individuals in building collections of resources appropriate to the developmental and maturity levels of students. These collections provide resources which support the curriculum and are consistent with the philosophy, goals, and objectives of the school district. Resources in school library media collections represent diverse points of view and current as well as historical issues.

While English is, by history and tradition, the customary language of the United States, the languages in use in any given community may vary. Schools serving communities in which other languages are used make efforts to accommodate the needs of students for whom English is a second language. To support these efforts, and to ensure equal access to resources and services, the school library media program provides resources which reflect the linguistic pluralism of the community.

Members of the school community involved in the collection development process employ educational criteria to select resources unfettered by their personal, political, social, or religious views. Students and educators served by the school library media program have access to resources and services free of constraints resulting from personal, partisan, or doctrinal disapproval. School library media professionals resist efforts by individuals to define what is appropriate for all students or teachers to read, view, or hear.

Major barriers between students and resources include: imposing age or grade level restrictions on the use of resources, limiting the use of interlibrary loan and access to electronic information, charging fees for information in specific formats, requiring permissions from parents or teachers, establishing restricted shelves or closed collections, and labeling. Policies, procedures, and rules related to the use of resources and services support free and open access to information.

The school board adopts policies that guarantee students access to a broad range of ideas. These include policies on collection development and procedures for the review of resources about which concerns have been raised. Such policies, developed by persons in the school community, provide for a timely and fair hearing and assure that procedures are applied equitably to all expressions of concern. School library media professionals implement district policies and procedures in the school.

Free Access to Libraries for Minors

An Interpretation of the Library Bill of Rights

The following is an interpretation of the Library Bill of Rights as it relates to free access to libraries for minors. It was adopted by the ALA Council in 1972 and amended in 1981 and 1991.

Library policies and procedures which effectively deny minors equal access to all library resources available to other users violate the Library Bill of Rights. The American Library Association opposes all attempts to restrict access to library services, materials, and facilities based on the age of library users.

Article 5 of the Library Bill of Rights states, "A person's right to use a library should not be denied or abridged because of origin, age, background, or views." The "right to use a library" includes free access to, and unrestricted use of, all the services, materials, and facilities the library has to offer. Every restriction on access to, and use of, library resources, based solely on the chronological age, educational level, or legal emancipation of users violates article 5.

Libraries are charged with the mission of developing resources to meet the diverse information needs and interests of the communities they serve. Services, materials, and facilities which fulfill the needs and interests of library users at different stages in their personal development are a necessary part of library resources. The needs and interests of each library user, and resources appropriate to meet those needs and interests, must be determined on an individual basis. Librarians cannot predict what resources will best fulfill the needs and interests of any individual user based on a single criterion such as chronological age, level of education, or legal emancipation.

The selection and development of library resources should not be diluted because of minors having the same access to library resources as adult users. Institutional self-censorship diminishes the credibility of the library in the community and restricts access for all library users.

Librarians and governing bodies should not resort to age restrictions on access to library resources in an effort to avoid actual or anticipated objections from parents or anyone else. The mission, goals, and objectives of libraries do not authorize librarians or governing bodies to assume, abrogate, or overrule the rights and responsibilities of parents or legal guardians. Librarians and governing bodies should maintain that parents—and only parents—have the right and the responsibility to restrict the access of their children—and only their children—to library resources. Parents or legal guardians who do not want their children to have access to certain library services, materials, or facilities should so advise their children. Librarians and governing bodies cannot assume the role of parents or the functions of parental authority in the private relationship between parent and child. Librarians and governing bodies have a public and professional obligation to provide equal access to all library resources for all library users.

Librarians have a professional commitment to ensure that all members of the community they serve have free and equal access to the entire range of library resources regardless of content, approach, format, or amount of detail. This principle of library service applies equally to all users, minors as well as adults. Librarians and governing bodies must uphold this principle in order to provide adequate and effective service to minors.

Diversity in Collection Development

An Interpretation of the Library Bill of Rights

The following is an interpretation of the Library Bill of Rights as it relates to diversity in development of a library and media collections. It was adopted by the American Library Association in 1982 and amended in 1990 by the ALA Council.

Throughout history, censors' aims have varied from generation to generation. Books and other materials have not been selected or have been removed from library collections for prejudicial language and ideas, political content, economic theory, social philosophy, religious beliefs, sexual expression, and other topics of a potentially controversial nature.

Some examples of censorship may include removing or not selecting materials because they are considered by some as racist or sexist; not purchasing conservative religious materials; not selecting materials about or by minorities because it is thought these groups or interests are not represented in a community; or not providing information on or materials from nonmainstream political entities.

Librarians may seek to increase user awareness of materials on various social concerns by many means, including, but not limited to, issuing bibliographies and presenting exhibits and programs.

Librarians have a professional responsibility to be inclusive, not exclusive, in collection development and in the provision of interlibrary loan. Access to all materials legally obtainable should be assured to the user, and policies should not unjustly exclude materials even if they are offensive to the librarian or the user. Collection development should reflect the philosophy inherent in article 2 of the Library Bill of Rights: "Libraries should provide materials and information presenting all points of view on current and historical issues. Materials should not be proscribed or removed because of partisan or doctrinal disapproval." A balanced collection reflects a diversity of materials, not an equality of numbers. Collection development responsibilities include selecting materials in the languages in common use in the community which the library serves. Collection development and the selection of materials should be done according to professional standards and established selection and review procedures.

There are many complex facets to any issue, and variations of context in which issues may be expressed, discussed, or interpreted. Librarians have a professional responsibility to be fair, just, and equitable and to give all library users equal protection in guarding against violation of the library patron's right to read, view, or listen to materials and resources protected by the First Amendment, no matter what the viewpoint of the author, creator, or selector. Librarians have an obligation to protect library collections from removal of materials based on personal bias or prejudice, and to select and support the access to materials on all subjects that meet, as closely as possible, the needs and interests of all persons in the community which the library serves. This includes materials that reflect political, economic, religious, social, minority, and sexual issues.

Intellectual freedom, the essence of equitable library services, provides for free access to all expressions of ideas through which any and all sides of a question, cause, or movement may be explored. Toleration is meaningless without tolerance for what some may consider detestable. Librarians cannot justly permit their own preferences to limit their degree of tolerance in collection development, because freedom is indivisible.

D

Tips and Samples
for Writing a Selection Policy*

Every school system should have a comprehensive policy on the selection of instructional materials. It should relate to and include all materials, e.g., textbooks, library books, periodicals, films, video cassettes, records, cassettes, and CDs. The reason should be obvious: haphazard patterns of acquisition will result in waste because some—perhaps many—materials will overlap in content, or will be unrelated to changing patterns of instruction.

A comprehensive policy on the selection of instructional materials will also enable school professionals to rationally explain the school program to the community. And, most important in a crisis, when there are complaints about social studies texts, human development materials in the media center, or fiction in the English class, the use of the "objectionable" item can more easily be explained.

A good policy on the selection of instructional materials will include basic sections on objectives, responsibility, criteria, procedures for selection, reconsideration of materials, policies on controversial materials, and other special areas of concern to your particular system.

---

*For further assistance or encouragement, please contact the Office for Intellectual Freedom of the American Library Association, 50 East Huron Street, Chicago, Illinois 60611, (312) 280-4223.

Basic Components of a Selection Policy

Objectives

In developing your policy, you should state in succinct terms what it is your system is trying to accomplish in its educational program, and, in somewhat more detail, the objectives of selection.

Your overarching goal may be very broad.

For the School District:

- Instructional materials are selected by the school district to implement, enrich, and support the educational program for the student. Materials must serve both the breadth of the curriculum and the needs and interests of individual students. It is the obligation of the district to provide for a wide range of abilities and to respect the diversity of many differing points of view. To this end, principles must be placed above personal opinion and reason above prejudice in the selection of materials of the highest quality and appropriateness.

For the Library Media Center:

- The main objective of our selection procedure is to provide the students with a wide range of educational materials on all levels of difficulty and in a variety of formats, with diversity of appeal, allowing for the presentation of many different points of view.

- The objective of the media center is to make available to faculty and students a collection of materials that will enrich and support the curriculum and meet the needs of the students and faculty served.

More specific goals should be established by professionals for each learning level.

The objectives for selection should reflect the specific goals of the instructional program. In the case of textbooks, the goals may vary from subject to subject. For example, in the sciences, one principal goal might be accuracy in terms of the latest scientific knowledge, and in history, balance in the presentation of conflicting points of view. In the case of materials in the library media center, the goals may include meeting individual learning needs abilities and learning styles, providing background materials to supplement classroom instruction, providing a broad range of materials on controversial issues to help students develop critical analytical skills, etc.

Responsibility for Selection

Your policy should name by professional position those persons who will have responsibility for selection of textbooks and other instructional materials.

In most states in the United States, the locally elected or appointed school board, by law, has broad powers and responsibilities in the selection of instructional materials. This authority should be delegated by policy to appropriate professionals for day-to-day exercise.

While selection of materials involves many people, including administrators, supervisors, teachers, library media specialists, students, and even community residents, the responsibility for coordinating and recommending the selection and purchase of library media materials should rest with the certificated library media personnel. Responsibility for coordinating the selection and purchase of textbooks and other classroom materials may rest with appropriate department chairpersons or with textbook or media evaluation committees.

Write into your policy under Responsibility for Selection (or similar title) exactly who is responsible for selection of materials, e.g., department heads, curriculum specialists, directors of curriculum and instruction, librarians or media specialists.

Sample statement of responsibility for the School District:

- The elected Board of Education shall delegate to the Superintendent of Schools the authority and responsibility for selection of all print and nonprint materials. Responsibilities for actual selection shall rest with appropriate professionally trained personnel who shall discharge this obligation consistent with the Board's adopted selection criteria and procedures. Selection procedures shall involve representatives of the professional staff directly affected by the selections, and persons qualified by preparation to aid in wise selection.

Sample statement of responsibility for the Library Media Center:

- The library media specialist will work cooperatively with staff members to interpret and guide the application of the policy in making day-to-day selections. Final responsibility for selection of materials for the library media center lies with the media specialists.

Criteria

In terms of the subject matter covered, your policy will include criteria, the application of criteria relevant to your objectives, excellence (artistic, literary, etc.), appropriateness to level of user, superiority in treatment of controversial issues, and ability to stimulate further intellectual and social development. Consider authenticity, appropriateness, interest, content, and circumstances of use.

You will probably want to include technical criteria in your policy, for example, clarity of sound in audio materials and cinematography in videocassette.

Specific criteria should be spelled out to guide all professionals involved in selection in deciding on specific items:

- Staff members involved in selection of resource materials shall use the following criteria as a guide:
  1. Educational significance
  2. Contribution the subject matter makes to the curriculum and to the interests of the students
  3. Favorable reviews found in standard selection sources
  4. Favorable recommendations based on preview and examination of materials by professional personnel
  5. Reputation and significance of the author, producer, and publisher
  6. Validity, currency, and appropriates of material
  7. Contribution the material makes to breath of representative viewpoints on controversial issues
  8. High degree of potential user appeal
  9. High artistic quality and/or literary style
  10. Quality and variety of format
  11. Value commensurate with cost and/or need
  12. Timeliness or permanence
  13. Integrity

- The following recommended lists shall be consulted in the selection of materials, but selection is not limited to their listings.
  1. Bibliographies (latest editions available, including supplements):
     American Historical Fiction
     Basic Book Collection for Elementary Grades
     The Best in Children's Books
     Children and Books
     Children's Catalog
     Elementary School Library Collection
     European Historical Fiction and Biography

Guide to Sources in Educational Media
Junior High School Catalog
Reference Books for School Libraries
Subject Guide to Children's Books in Print
Subject Index to Books for Intermediate Grades
Subject Index to Books for Primary Grades
Westinghouse Learning Directory
and as a part of the vertical file index, other special bibliographies, many of which have been prepared by educational organizations for particular subject matter areas.

2. Current reviewing media:
AASA Science Books and Films
American Film & Video Association Evaluations
Booklist
Bulletin of the Center for Children's Books
Horn Book
Kirkus Reviews
Library Journal
School Library Journal
Wilson Library Bulletin

- The following criteria will be used as they apply:
  1. Learning resources shall support and be consistent with the general educational goals of the state and district and the aims and objectives of individual schools and specific courses.
  2. Learning resources shall meet high standards of quality in factual content and presentation.
  3. Learning resources shall be appropriate for the subject area and for the age, emotional development, ability level, learning styles and social development of the students for whom the materials are selected.
  4. Physical format and appearance of learning resources shall be suitable for their intended use.
  5. Learning resources shall be designed to help students gain an awareness of our pluralistic society.
  6. Learning resources shall be designed to motivate students and staff to examine their own duties, responsibilities, rights and privileges as participating citizens in our society.
  7. Learning resources shall be selected for their strengths rather than rejected for their weaknesses.

The selection of learning resources on controversial issues will be directed towards maintaining a diverse collection representing various views.

Learning resources shall clarify historical and contemporary forces by presenting and analyzing intergroup tension and conflict objectively, placing emphasis on recognizing and understanding social and economic problems.

- The following kinds of material should be selected for the media center:
  1. Materials which are an integral part of the instructional program.
  2. Materials which are appropriate for the reading level and understanding of students in the school.
  3. Materials which reflect the interests and needs of the students and faculty served by the media center.
  4. Materials which merit inclusion in the collection because of their literary and/or artistic value.
  5. Materials which present information with the greatest degree of accuracy and clarity possible.
  6. Materials which represent a fair and unbiased presentation of information. In controversial areas, the media specialist in cooperation with the faculty should select materials representing as many shades of opinion as possible in order that students may have available varying viewpoints.

Procedures

Your procedures should describe all steps from initial screening to final selection. They should also include provisions for coordination among departments and professionals working at different learning levels, etc.; for handling recommendations from other faculty and students; and for the review of existing materials (for possible replacement, etc.).

Include at least a partial list of selection aids such as lists of reviewing sources (if not included in preceding section). You may also want to list sources which should not be used.

This will be a large part of your selection policy. It is important to list the type of materials you collect, why you need them, and how you obtain them. Include here your policies on reevaluation (weeding), replacing and repairing materials, etc.

Sample procedure statements:

1. In selecting learning resources, professional personnel will evaluate available resources and curriculum needs and will consult reputable, professionally prepared aids to selection and other appropriate sources. The actual resource will be examined whenever possible.
2. Recommendations for purchase involve administrators, teachers, students, district personnel, and community persons, as appropriate.
3. Gift materials shall be judged by the criteria outlined and shall be accepted or rejected by those criteria.
4. Selection is an ongoing process which should include the removal of materials no longer appropriate and the replacement of lost and worn materials still of educational value.

or

5. Requests, suggestions, and reactions for the purchase of instructional materials shall be gathered from staff to the greatest extent possible and students when appropriate.
6. Reviews of proposed acquisitions will be sought in the literature of reputable professional organizations and other reviewing sources recognized for their objectivity and wide experience.
7. Materials will be examined by professional staff to the extent necessary or practicable to apply criteria. Preview copies are available for on-site examination by the public upon written request to the District Director of Instruction.
8. Textbooks will be selected after examination by a representative committee of teachers, principals, curriculum specialists, directors of instruction, and others who have professional expertise in objective evaluation of materials.
9. Materials for the District Film and Video Center will be selected by preview committees, curriculum specialists, and through use of professional review sources.
10. Building media center materials selection will be coordinated by the building media specialists, or the principal, where there is no professional staff, involving teachers and curriculum specialists.
11. Area Advisory Councils may be used to review materials recommended by professional selection committees.

or

Materials for media centers are selected by the professional media staff with due regard to suggestions from the faculty, parents, and students.

Final selection is made by the media specialists of the school in which the center is housed. Professionally recognized reviewing periodicals, standard catalogs, and other selection aids are used by the media specialists and the faculty to guide them in their selection.

Special Areas

Some miscellaneous items to consider in your policy are gifts, sponsored materials, expensive materials, ephemeral materials, jobbers and salespersons, locked case, special requests, etc., free and inexpensive materials, professional materials, and procedure for handling lost materials. Do you charge fines, maintain special collections not available to all patrons (e.g., a collection of materials for teachers only), handle special requests? These "special concerns" can be outlined in this section of your policy. Make sure to include your procedures for integrating gifts and sponsored materials. Usually, it is stated that criteria for inclusion of gifts and sponsored materials are the same as for purchased materials.

Policies on Controversial Materials

Here, or in another place in your policy, you should include a statement on intellectual freedom and why it is important to maintain. You may wish to include the test of the First Amendment to the United States Constitution—"Congress shall make no law respecting an establishment of religion, or prohibiting the free exercise thereof; or abridging the freedom of speech, or of the press; or the right of the people peaceable to assemble, and to petition the Government for a redress of grievances," and the Library Bill of Rights. (A copy is included at the end of this in chapter 1.)

Sample Statement on intellectual freedom:

* The school board subscribes in principle to the statements of policy on library philosophy as expressed in the American Library Association Library Bill of Rights, a copy of which is appended to and made a part of this policy.

Reconsideration

Occasional objections to instructional materials will be made despite the quality of the selection process; therefore, the procedure for handling reconsideration of challenged materials in response to questions concerning their appropriateness should be stated. This procedure should establish the framework for registering a complaint that provides for a hearing with appropriate action while defending the principles of freedom of information, the student's right to access of materials, and the professional responsibility and integrity of the school faculty. The principles of intellectual freedom are inherent in the First Amendment of the Constitution of the United States and are expressed in the Library Bill of Rights adopted by the Council of the American Library Association. In the event instructional materials are questioned, the principles of intellectual freedom should be defended rather than the materials.

List here the specific steps that will be taken when you are asked to reconsider materials in your collection. These steps should include:

- asking the complainant to fill out a written complaint form.
- assigning a review committee to examine the material in question.
- requesting that the committee report their findings to the school board.

The procedure for handling complaints should describe every step from the initial response to the complaint through the highest appeal.

Procedure for Handling Complaints

No duly selected materials whose appropriateness is challenged shall be removed from the school except upon the recommendation of a review committee (as provided for below) with the concurrence of the Superintendent or, upon the Superintendent's recommendation, the concurrence of the Board of Education, or upon formal action of the Board of Education when a recommendation of a review committee is appealed to it.

Procedures to be observed:

1. All complaints to staff members shall be reported to the building principal involved, whether received by telephone, letter, or in personal conversation.
2. The principal shall contact the complainant to discuss the complaint and attempt to resolve it informally by explaining the philosophy and goals of the school district and/or the library media center.

3. If the complaint is not resolved informally, the complainant shall be supplied with a packet of materials consisting of the District's instructional goals and objectives, materials selection policy statement, and the procedure for handling objections. This packet will also include a standard printed form which shall be completed and returned before consideration will be given to the complaint.

4. If the formal request for reconsideration has not been received by the principal within two weeks, it shall be considered closed. If the request is returned, the reasons for selection of the specific work shall be reestablished by the appropriate staff.

5. In accordance with statement of philosophy, no questioned materials shall be removed from the school pending a final decision. Pending the outcome of the request for reconsideration, however, access to questioned materials can be denied to the child (or children) of the parents making the complaint, if they so desire.

6. Upon receipt of a completed objection form, the principal in the building involved will call together a committee of five to consider the complaint. This committee shall consist of the curriculum director and from the school involved: the principal, the library media center director, a teacher, and a PTA representative.

7. The committee shall meet to discuss the material, following the guidelines set forth in Instructions to Evaluation Committee and shall prepare a report on the material containing their recommendations on disposition of the matter.

8. The principal shall notify complainant of the decision and send a formal report and recommendation to the Superintendent. In answering the complainant, the principal shall explain the book selection system, give the guidelines used for selection, and cite authorities used in reaching decisions. If the committee decides to keep the work that caused the complaint, the complainant shall be given an explanation. If the complaint is valid, the principal will acknowledge it and make recommended changes.

9. If the complainant is still not satisfied, he/she may ask the Superintendent to present an appeal to the Board of Education which shall make a final determination of the issue. The Board of Education may seek assistance from outside organizations such as the American Library Association, the Association for Supervision and Curriculum Development, etc., in making its determination.

Sample Letter to Complainant

Dear _____:

We appreciate your concern over the use of _____ in our school district. The district has developed procedures for selecting materials, but realizes that not everyone will agree with every selection made.

To help you understand the selection process, we are sending copies of the district's:

1. Instructional goals and objectives
2. Materials Selection Policy statement
3. Procedure for Handling Objections

If you are still concerned after you review this material, please complete the Request for Reconsideration of Material form and return it to me. You may be assured of prompt attention to your request. If I have not heard from you within two weeks, we will assume you no longer wish to file a formal complaint.

Sincerely,

Principal

Instructions to Evaluating Committee

- Bear in mind the principles of the freedom to learn and to read and base your decision on these broad principles rather than on defense of individual materials. Freedom of inquiry is vital to education in a democracy.

- Study thoroughly all materials referred to you and read available reviews. The general acceptance of the materials should be checked by consulting standard evaluation aids and local holdings in other schools.

- Passages or parts should not be pulled out of context. The values and faults should be weighed against each other and the opinions based on the materials as a whole.

- Your report, presenting both majority and minority opinions, will be presented by the principal to the complainant at the conclusion of our discussion of the questioned material.

Statement of Concern about Library/Media Center Resources

This is where you identify who in your own structure has authorized use of this form—Director, Board of Trustees, Board of Education, etc.—and to whom to return form.

Date _____

Name _____

Address _____

City _____ State _____ Zip _____

Phone # _____

1. Resource on which you are commenting:

   _____ Book   _____ Audiovisual Resource

   _____ Magazine   _____ Content of Library Program

   _____ Newspaper   _____ Other

   Title _____

   Author/Producer _____

2. What brought this title to your attention?

3. Please comment on the resource as a whole as well as being specific on those matters which concern you. (Use other side if needed.)

   Comment:

Optional:
4. What resource(s) do you suggest to provide additional information on this topic?

Revised by the ALA Intellectual Freedom Committee, January 12, 1983.

Guidelines for Student Publications

Following are model guidelines for student publications prepared by the Student Press Law Center. First published in 1985, the guidelines were revised to reflect the impact of the United States Supreme Court's Hazelwood *decision in 1990.*

Preamble: The following guidelines are based on state and federal court decisions that have determined the First Amendment rights of students, including the Supreme Court's decision in *Hazelwood School District v. Kuhlmeier* (1988). These guidelines do not provide a legal basis for school officials or employees to exercise prior restraint or prior review of student publications. The Student Press Law Center cautions that court rulings indicate that policies which provide for prior review and restraint and meet constitutional requirements of precision, narrow scope and protection of speech are almost impossible to develop for forum publications.

In addition, schools that adopt a prior review and/or prior restraint policy assume legal liability for the content of the publications, whether they are school-sponsored or nonschool-sponsored. Court decisions indicate that a school likely will be protected from liability if by written policy it rejects prior review and prior restraint.

I. Statement of Policy

It is undeniable that students are protected in their exercise of freedom of expression by the First Amendment to the Constitution of the United States. Accordingly, school officials are responsible for ensuring freedom of expression for all students.

It is the policy of the _____ Board of Education that (*newspaper*), (*yearbook*) and (*literary magazine*), the official, school-sponsored publications of _____ High School have been established as forums for student expression and as voices in the uninhibited, robust, free and open discussion of issues. Each publication should provide a full opportunity for students to inquire, question and exchange ideas. Content should reflect all areas of student interest, including topics about which there may be dissent or controversy.

It is the policy of the _____ Board of Education that student journalists shall have the right to determine the content of official student publications. Accordingly, the following guidelines relate only to establishing grounds for disciplinary actions subsequent to publication.

II. Official School Publications

A. **Responsibilities of Student Journalists**

Students who work on official student publications determine the content of those publications and are responsible for that content. These students should:
1. Determine the content of the student publication;
2. Strive to produce a publication based upon professional standards of accuracy, objectivity and fair play;
3. Review material to improve sentence structure, grammar, spelling and punctuation;
4. Check and verify all facts and verify the accuracy of all quotations; and
5. In the case of editorials or letters to the editor concerning controversial issues, determine the need for rebuttal comments and opinions and provide space therefore if appropriate.

B. **Prohibited Material**

1. Students cannot publish or distribute material that is "obscene as to minors." "Minor" means any person under the age of 18.

Obscene as to minors is defined as material that meets *all three* of the following requirements:

(a) the average person, applying contemporary community standards, would find that the publication, taken as a whole, appeals to a minor's prurient interest in sex; and

(b) the publication depicts or describes, in a patently offensive way, sexual conduct such as ultimate sexual acts (normal or perverted), masturbation and lewd exhibition of the genitals; and

(c) the work, taken as a whole, lacks serious literary, artistic, political or scientific value.

Indecent or vulgar language is not obscene.

[Note: Many statutes exist defining what is "obscene as to minors." If such a statute is in force in your state, it should be substituted in place of Section II (B)(1).]

2. Students cannot publish or distribute libelous material. Libelous statements are provably false and unprivileged statements that do demonstrated injury to an individual's or business's reputation in the community. If the allegedly libeled party is a "public figure" or "public official" as defined below, then school officials must show that the false statement was published "with actual malice," *i.e.,* that the student journalists knew that the statement was false or that they published it with reckless disregard for the truth—without trying to verify the truthfulness of the statement.

    (a) A public official is a person who holds an elected or appointed public office.

    (b) A public figure either seeks the public's attention or is well known because of personal achievements.

    (c) School employees are public officials or public figures in articles concerning their school-related activities.

    (d) When an allegedly libelous statement concerns a private individual, school officials must show that the false statement was published willfully or negligently, *i.e.,* the student journalist who wrote or published the statement has failed to exercise reasonably prudent care.

    (e) Under the "fair comment rule," a student is free to express an opinion on a matter of public interest. Specifically, a student may criticize school policy or the performance of teachers, administrators, school officials and other school employees.

3. Students cannot publish or distribute material that will cause "a material and substantial disruption of school activities."

(a) Disruption is defined as student rioting; unlawful seizures of property; destruction of property; or substantial student participation in a school boycott, sit-in, walk-out or other related form of activity. Material such as racial, religious or ethnic slurs, however distasteful, are not in and of themselves disruptive under these guidelines. Threats of violence are not materially disruptive without some act in furtherance of that threat or a reasonable belief and expectation that the author of the threat has the capability and intent of carrying through on that threat in a fashion not permitting acts other than suppression of speech to mitigate the threat in a timely manner. *Material that stimulates heated discussion or debate does not constitute the type of disruption prohibited.*

(b) For a student publication to be considered disruptive, specific facts must exist upon which one could reasonably forecast that a likelihood of immediate, substantial material disruption to normal school activity would occur if the material were further distributed or has occurred as a result of the material's distribution. Mere undifferentiated fear or apprehension of disturbance is not enough; school administrators must be able affirmatively to show substantial facts that reasonably support a forecast of likely disruption.

(c) In determining whether a student publication is disruptive, consideration must be given to the context of this distribution as well as the content of the material. In this regard, consideration should be given to past experience in the school with similar material, past experience in the school dealing with and supervising the students in the school, current events influencing student attitudes and behavior and whether there have been any instances of actual or threatened disruption prior to or contemporaneously with the dissemination of the student publication in question.

(d) School officials must protect advocates of unpopular viewpoints.

(e) "School activity" means educational student activity sponsored by the school and includes, by way of example and not by way of limitation, classroom work, library activities, physical education classes, official assemblies and other similar gatherings, school athletic contests, band concerts, school plays and scheduled in-school lunch periods.

C. **Legal Advice**

1. If, in the opinion of student editor, student editorial staff or faculty adviser, material proposed for publication may be "obscene," "libelous" or would cause an "immediate, material and substantial disruption of school activities," the legal opinion of a practicing attorney should be sought. The services of the attorney for the local newspaper or the free legal services of the Student Press Law Center (202-466-5242) are recommended.
2. Legal fees charged in connection with the consultation will be paid by the board of education.
3. The final decision of whether the material is to be published will be left to the student editor or student editorial staff.

III. Nonschool-Sponsored Publications

School officials may not ban the distribution of nonschool-sponsored publications on school grounds. However, students who violate any rule listed under II(B) may be disciplined after distribution.

1. School officials may regulate the time, place and manner of distribution.
   (a) Nonschool-sponsored publications will have the same rights of distribution as official school publications;
   (b) "Distribution" means dissemination of a publication to students at a time and place of normal school activity, or immediately prior or subsequent thereto, by means of handing out free copies, selling or offering copies for sale, accepting donations for copies of the publication in areas of the school which are generally frequented by students.
2. School officials cannot:
   (a) Prohibit the distribution of anonymous literature or require that literature bear the name of the sponsoring organization or author;
   (b) Ban the distribution of literature because it contains advertising;
   (c) Ban the sale of literature; or
   (d) Create regulations that discriminate against nonschool-sponsored publications or interfere with the effective distribution of sponsored or nonsponsored publications.

IV. Protected Speech

School officials cannot:

1. Ban speech solely because it is controversial, takes extreme, "fringe" or minority opinions, or is distasteful, unpopular or unpleasant;
2. Ban the publication or distribution of material relating to sexual issues including, but not limited to, virginity, birth control and sexually transmitted diseases (including AIDS);
3. Censor or punish the occasional use of indecent, vulgar or so-called "four-letter" words in student publications;
4. Prohibit criticism of the policies, practices or performance of teachers, school officials, the school itself or of any public officials;
5. Cut off funds to official student publications because of disagreement over editorial policy;
6. Ban speech that merely advocates illegal conduct without proving that such speech is directed toward and will actually cause imminent unlawful action;
7. Ban the publication or distribution of material written by non-students;
8. Prohibit the school newspaper from accepting advertising; or
9. Prohibit the endorsement of candidates for student office or for public office at any level.

V. Commercial Speech

Advertising is a constitutionally protected expression. School publications may accept advertising. Acceptance or rejection of advertising is within the purview of the publication staff, who may accept any ads except for those for products or services that are illegal for all students. Political ads may be accepted. The publication should not accept ads only on one side of an issue of election.

VI. Adviser Job Security

The adviser is not a censor. No teacher who advises a student publication will be fired, transferred or removed from the advisership by reason of his or her refusal to exercise editorial control over the student publication or to otherwise suppress the protected free expression of student journalists.

VII. Prior Restraint

No student publication, whether nonschool-sponsored or official, will be reviewed by school administrators prior to distribution or withheld from distribution. The school assumes no liability for the content of any student publication, and urges all student journalists to recognize that with editorial control comes responsibility, including the responsibility to follow professional journalism standards.

VIII. Circulation

These guidelines will be included in the handbook on student rights and responsibilities and circulated to all students.

Tips for Dealing with Concerns about Library Resources

As with any public service, libraries receive complaints and expressions of concern. One of the librarian's responsibilities is to handle these complaints in a respectful and fair manner. The complaints that librarians often worry about the most are those dealing with library resources or free access policies. The key to successfully handling these complaints is to be sure the library staff and the governing authorities are all knowledgeable about the complaint procedures and their implementation. As normal operating procedure, each library should:

1. **Maintain a materials selection policy.** It should be in written form and approved by the appropriate governing authority. It should apply to all library materials equally.

2. **Maintain a library service policy.** This should cover registration policies, programming, and services in the library that involve access issues.

3. **Maintain a clearly defined method for handling complaints.** The complaint must be filed in writing and the complainant must be properly identified before action is taken. A decision should be deferred until fully considered by appropriate administrative authority. The process should be followed, whether the complaint originates internally or externally.

4. **Maintain inservice training.** Conduct periodic inservice training to acquaint staff, administration, and the governing authority with the materials selection policy and library service policy and procedures for handling complaints.

5. **Maintain lines of communication with civic, religious, educational, and political bodies of the community.** Library board and staff participation in local civic organizations and presentations to these organizations should emphasize the library's selection process and intellectual freedom principles.

6. **Maintain a vigorous public information program on behalf of intellectual freedom.** Newspapers, radio, and television should be informed of policies governing resource selection and use, and of any special activities pertaining to intellectual freedom.

7. **Maintain familiarity with any local municipal and state legislation pertaining to intellectual freedom and First Amendment rights.** Following these practices will not preclude receiving complaints from pressure groups or individuals, but should provide a base from which to operate when these concerns are expressed. When a complaint is made, follow one or more of the steps listed below:

   (a) Listen calmly and courteously to the complaint. Remember the person has a right to express a concern. Use of good communication skills helps many people understand the need for diversity in library collections and the use of library resources. In the event the person is not satisfied, advise the complainant of the library policy and procedures for handling library resource statements of concern. If a person does fill out a form about their concern, make sure a prompt written reply related to the concern is sent.

   (b) It is essential to notify the administration and/or the governing authority (library board, etc.) of the complaint and assure them that the library's procedures are being followed. Present full, written information giving the nature of the complaint and identifying the source.

   (c) When appropriate, seek the support of the local media. Freedom to read and freedom of the press go hand in hand.

   (d) When appropriate, inform local civic organizations of the facts and enlist their support. Meet negative pressure with positive pressure.

(e) Assert the principles of the Library Bill of Rights as a professional responsibility. Laws governing obscenity, subversive material, and other questionable matter are subject to interpretation by courts. Library materials found to meet the standards set in the materials selection policy should not be removed from public access until after an adversary hearing resulting in a final judicial determination.

(f) Contact the ALA Office for Intellectual Freedom and your state intellectual freedom committee to inform them of the complaint and to enlist their support and the assistance of other agencies.

The principles and procedures discussed above apply to all kinds of resource-related complaints or attempts to censor and are supported by groups such as the National Education Association, the American Civil Liberties Union, the National Council of Teachers of English, as well as the American Library Association. While the practices provide positive means for preparing for and meeting pressure group complaints, they serve the more general purpose of supporting the Library Bill of Rights, particularly Article 3 which states that: "Libraries should challenge censorship in the fulfillment of their responsibility to provide information and enlightenment."

Source: Office for Intellectual Freedom, American Library Association Revised by the ALA Intellectual Freedom Committee, 1983

Selected List of Concerned National Organizations

American Library Association
  Office for Intellectual Freedom
  50 East Huron Street
  Chicago, IL 60611
  Phone: 312/280-4223
  Fax: 312/440-9374

American Association of School
  Administrators
  1801 N. Monroe Street
  Arlington, VA 22209
  Phone: 703/528-0700
  Fax: 703/841-1543

American Association of School
  Libraries
  50 E. Huron Street
  Chicago, IL 60611
  Phone: 312/280-4386
  Fax: 312/664-7459

American Federation of Teachers
  555 New Jersey Ave., N.W.
  Washington, DC 20001
  Phone: 202/879-4400

American Civil Liberties Union
  132 W. 43rd Street
  New York, NY 10036
  Phone 212/944-9800
  Fax: 212/869-9068

Americans for Religious Liberty
  P.O. Box 6656
  Silver Spring, MD 20916
  Phone: 301/598-2447

Americans United for Separation
  of Church and State
  900 Silver Spring Ave.
  Silver Spring, MD 20910
  Phone: 301/588-2282
  Fax: 301/495-9173

The Association for Supervision
  and Curriculum Development
  1250 N. Pitt Street
  Alexandria, VA 22314
  Phone: 703/549-9110

Council of Chief State School
  Officers
  1 Massachusetts Ave., N.W.
  Suite 700
  Washington, DC 20001-1431
  Phone: 202/408-5505
  Fax: 202/408-8072

Freedom to Read Foundation
  50 E. Huron Street
  Chicago, IL 60611
  Phone: 312/280-4226

International Reading
  Association
  800 Barksdale Road
  P.O. Box 8139
  Newark, DE 19714-8139
  Phone: 302/731-1600

National Association of Biology
  Teachers
  11250 Roger Bacon Drive, #19
  Reston, VA 22090
  Phone: 703/471-1134

National Center for Science
  Education
  P.O. Box 9477
  Berkeley, CA 94709-9953
  Phone: 415/528-2521

National Coalition Against
  Censorship
  275 7th Ave.
  New York, NY 10001
  Phone: 212/807-6222

National Council for Social
  Studies
  3501 Newark Street, N.W.
  Washington, DC 20016
  Phone: 202/966-7840
  Fax: 202/966-2061

National Council of Teachers of
  English
  1111 Kenyon Road
  Urbana, IL 61801
  Phone: 217/328-3870
  Fax: 217/328-9645

National Council on Religion and
  Public Education
  Charles Kniker
  N155 Lagomarcino Hall
  Iowa State University
  Ames, IA 50011
  Phone: 515/294-7925

National Education Association
  Human and Civil Rights
  Division
  1201 16th Street, N.W.
  Washington, DC 20036
  Phone: 202/822-7700
  Fax: 202/822-7578

National School Boards
  Association
  1680 Duke Street
  Alexandria, VA 22314
  Phone: 703/838-6722

People for the American Way
  2000 M Street N.W., Suite 400
  Washington, DC 20036
  Phone: 202/467-4999
  Fax: 202/293-2672

K

Summaries of
Selected Legal Cases

Tinker v. Des Moines Independent Community School District, 393 U.S. 503 (1969)

The *Tinker* case arose when a group of students decided to publicize their objection to the Vietnam War and their support for a truce by wearing black armbands in school during the 1967 holiday season. When the principals of the Des Moines schools became aware of the students' intentions, they announced that any student wearing an armband would be asked to remove it and if the request were refused, the student would be suspended until he or she returned without the armband.

A number of students, among them John and Mary Beth Tinker and Christopher Eckhardt (15, 13, and 16, respectively), went ahead with their plans and wore the armbands to school. There was no disturbance or disruption of normal school activities but, nevertheless, the students were told to remove their armbands in accordance with the principals' edict. When they refused, they were ordered to leave school. They returned to school two weeks later, sans armbands; but in the meantime, they had filed suit in federal court.

The Tinkers and Eckhardt lost their case at both the district court level and in the United States Court of Appeals. The U.S. Supreme Court, however, reversed these decisions. The majority opinion pointed out in February 1969 that neither students nor teachers "shed their Constitutional right to freedom of speech or expression at the schoolhouse gate." The Court held that the First Amendment protects the rights of public school children to express their political and social views during school hours. The decision held further that school officials may not place arbitrary curbs on student speech in the public schools. It is particularly interesting to note that while many individuals had taken for granted that school children did have First Amendment rights of free speech, the Supreme Court had never directly said so prior to this case.

Presidents Council, District 25 v. Community School Board No. 25 (New York City), 457 F.2d 289 (2d Cir. 1972), 409 U.S. 998 (1972)

This 1972 case was the first to consider whether a school board could remove books from a school library. At issue was a school board action revoking library access by junior high school students to *Down These Mean Streets,* by Piri Thomas, an autobiographical account of a Puerto Rican growing up in Spanish Harlem. The book's language and graphic sexual scenes offended some people in the community, who requested its removal.

The opinion of the U.S. Court of Appeals for the Second Circuit reflected the traditional deference to school board discretion by upholding its action revoking free access to Thomas' novel. Bypassing the constitutional aspects of the case, the court reduced the issue to one of shelving a book: "To suggest that the shelving or unshelving of books presents a constitutional issue, particularly when there is no showing of a curtailment of freedom of speech or thought, is a proposition we cannot accept." Judge Mulligan, writing for the court, declared that someone has to bear responsibility for book selection, and since school boards are statutorily empowered to operate the schools and prescribe the curriculum, the board is the appropriate body.

Minarcini v. Strongsville (Ohio) City School District, 541 F.2d 577 (6th Cir. 1976)

This suit was prompted by the Strongsville City Board of Education's rejection of faculty recommendations to approve the purchase of Joseph Heller's *Catch-22* and Kurt Vonnegut's *God Bless You, Mr. Rosewater* for use in the high school curriculum. The school board also ordered two books, *Catch-22* and Vonnegut's *Cat's Cradle*, removed from the library. No official reason was given for the removal; the only apparent explanation was contained in the minutes of a board meeting at which the books were described as "completely sick" and "garbage."

In 1976, the U.S. Court of Appeals for the Sixth Circuit ruled against the school board, upholding the students' First Amendment right to receive information and the librarians' right to disseminate it. Judge Edward, writing for the court, rejected the absolute right of a school board to remove from the library any book it might regard with disfavor:

> A library is a storehouse of knowledge. When created for a public school, it is an important privilege created by the state for the benefit of students in the schools. That privilege is not subject to being withdrawn by succeeding school boards whose members might desire to "winnow" the library for books the contents of which occasioned their displeasure or disapproval.

The court further emphasized that the responsibility of the board to provide access to material could not be minimized by the availability of the books in sources outside the school.

Right to Read Defense Committee v. School Committee of the City of Chelsea, 454 F. Supp. 703 (D. Mass. 1978)

In 1976, the banning of a poetry anthology, *Male and Female Under 18,* by the Chelsea (Massachusetts) School Committee was challenged in federal court. Plaintiffs were Chelsea school librarian Sonja Coleman and a group organized to support her, the Right to Read Defense Committee of Chelsea.

The action against *Male and Female Under 18* reflected the school committee's strong dislike of one poem in the anthology, "The City to a Young Girl," by Jody Caravaglia.

The school committee argued that under Massachusetts law the school committee has clear authority to approve or disapprove works used in the schools. In addition, the committee argued that it had legally decided not to include sex education in the curriculum and that, "The City to a Young Girl" represented an effort to introduce the subject improperly.

The Right to Read Defense Committee contended that *Male and Female Under 18* is fully protected by the First Amendment, that students possess a right to have access to materials fully protected by the First Amendment, and that the school committee's objections to the poem as "vulgar and offensive" could not constitutionally justify its suppression.

In July 1978, U.S. District Judge Joseph L. Tauro enjoined the school committee "from removing, or causing to be removed, in whole or in part," the anthology, which was to be made available to students "in accordance with standard library procedures." Relying particularly on the *Minarcini* precedent, Judge Tauro held that the committee's attempt to ban "The City to a Young Girl" could not pass First Amendment standards established by Supreme Court and lower court rulings.

Bicknell v. *Vergennes Union High School Board,* 475 F. Supp. 615 (D. Vt. 1979), 638 F.2d 438 (2d Cir. 1980)

In this Vermont case, litigated in 1979, U.S. District Court Judge Albert W. Coffin dismissed a complaint filed by librarian Elizabeth Phillips, several students, and others to protest the board's removal of *The Wanderer* and *Dog Day Afternoon* from the library; the imposition of a freeze on new library acquisitions; and the board's policy of screening all major acquisitions.

The court held that school boards have final authority in such matters and that the restrictions did not violate the constitutional rights of students or librarians:

> Although the court does not entirely agree with the policies and actions of the defendants, we do not find that those policies and actions directly or sharply infringe upon the basic constitutional rights of the students of Vergennes Union High School.
> ... the detailed procedures set forth for removing works from the collection obviously condition the general statements of the rights of those persons affected by the policy. Furthermore, the right of professional personnel under that policy "to freely select" materials for the collection are explicitly limited by the phrase "in accordance with Board policy."

In October 1980, the United States Court of Appeals for the Second Circuit, in a 2–1 decision, affirmed the dismissal.

Loewen v. *Turnipseed,* 488 F. Supp. 1138 (N.D. Miss. 1980)

A ninth-grade history textbook, *Mississippi: Conflict and Change,* by James W. Loewen and Charles Sallis, became a subject of controversy in 1974 when the Mississippi Textbook Purchasing Board refused to approve it for use in Mississippi public schools. The textbook committee, which can approve up to five history texts, selected only a revised version of the book used in ninth-grade classrooms in Mississippi for nearly two decades.

Loewen charged that the approved book "stigmatizes black people" and fails to mention or gives only passing reference to renowned Mississippi blacks. The five white members of the textbook committee rejected *Conflict and Change* on the grounds that it was too concerned with racial matters and too controversial; the two black members of the committee judged it suitable.

A suit was brought before U.S. District Judge Orma R. Smith, who ruled that the criteria used for selecting textbooks by the Mississippi committee were not justifiable grounds for rejecting *Mississippi: Conflict and Change.* Judge Smith held that because the controversial racial material in the book was a factor leading to its rejection, the plaintiff authors had been denied their constitutionally guaranteed rights of freedom of speech and of the press.

Zykan v. Warsaw (Indiana) Community School Corporation and Warsaw School Board of Trustees, 631 F.2d 1300 (7th Cir. 1980)

At issue was a curriculum review conducted by the school board in 1977, which resulted in the discontinuance of certain courses, the removal of some books from the curriculum, the dismissal of several teachers, and the discontinuance of publication of the high school newspaper. A high school student brought suit seeking to reverse school officials' decision to "limit or prohibit the use of certain textbooks, to remove a certain book from the school library, and to delete certain courses from the curriculum."

The district court dismissed Zykan's suit, which charged that school officials had violated constitutional guarantees of academic freedom and the "right to know." The case was then appealed to the U.S. Court of Appeals for the Seventh Circuit, which ruled that the school board has the right to establish a curriculum on the basis of its own discretion, but that it is forbidden to impose a "pall of orthodoxy" on the classroom. The right of students to file legal complaints about the school curriculum was recognized; however, the court held that the claims of students "must cross a relatively high threshold before entering upon the field of a constitutional claim suitable for federal court litigation."

Seyfried v. Walton, 668 F.2d 214 (3d Cir. 1981)

After rehearsals had begun for a student production of the musical "Pippin," that had been edited to remove certain sexually explicit scenes, the superintendent cancelled the play because of its remaining sexual content. Several students and parents sued, alleging the violation of the students' free expression rights. The Court of Appeals upheld the play's cancellation, finding that the school's sponsorship of a play would be viewed as an endorsement of the ideas it contained and that the school cannot be forced to promote a viewpoint at a variance with its educational mission. Student expression was not violated, the court concluded, since the script, unedited, was available in the school library, and no one was punished or reprimanded for any expression of ideas.

Pratt v. Independent School District No. 831, 670 F.2d 771 (8th Cir. 1982)

After parents and other citizens complained about the violence portrayed and the story's impact on students' religious and family values, a Minnesota school board removed a film version of "The Lottery" by Shirley Jackson and a related film trailer from the curriculum after five years' use. The film was about a small town in which one person was selected to be stoned to death each year. The trailer discussed the story and its themes. Three students sued to have the film reinstated in the curriculum.

The Court of Appeals upheld the students' challenge finding that the film was eliminated because of its "ideological content" in contravention of the First Amendment. It did not save the school board that the short story remained available in the school library in printed form and as a photographic recording. The court acknowledged the school board's broad discretion over curriculum, but stated that "[w]hat is at stake is the right to receive information and to be exposed to controversial ideas—a fundamental First Amendment right. If these films can be banned by those opposed to their ideological theme, then a precedent is set for the removal of any such work."

Board of Education, Island Trees Union Free School District No. 26 v. Pico, 457 U.S. 853 (1982)

In September 1975, three school board members sought removal of a number of books they had been informed were objectionable by a politically conservative organization. The following February, the board gave an "unofficial direction" that the books be removed from the school libraries, so that board members might read them. When the board's action attracted press attention, members responded with a press release describing the books as "anti-American, anti-Christian, anti-Semitic, and just plain filthy." The nine books that were the subject of the lawsuit were: *Slaughterhouse Five,* by Kurt Vonnegut, Jr.; *The Naked Ape,* by Desmond Morris; *Down These Mean Streets,* by Piri Thomas; *Best Short Stories of Negro Writers,* edited by Langston Hughes; *Go Ask Alice,* written anonymously; *Laughing Boy,* by Oliver LaFarge; *Black Boy,* by Richard Wright; *A Hero Ain't Nothin' But A Sandwich,* by Alice Childress; and *Soul on Ice* by Eldrige Cleaver.

The board appointed a review committee that recommended that five of the books be returned to the library shelves, two be placed on restricted shelves, and two be removed entirely from the library. No recommendation was made as to the final book. The full board then voted to remove all but one book, without explaining its action.

In a 5–4 decision, the Supreme Court upheld the students' challenge to this action. A clear majority of the Court held that school boards do not have unrestricted authority to select library books and that the First Amendment is implicated when books are removed arbitrarily. "If petitioners *intended* by their removal decision to deny respondents access to ideas with which petitioners disagreed, and if this intent was the decisive factor in petitioners' decision," Justice William Brennan wrote in a plurality opinion, "then petitioners have exercised their discretion in violation of the Constitution. To permit such intentions to control official actions would be to encourage the precise sort of officially prescribed orthodoxy unequivocally condemned [by this Court before]."

The majority of the Court condemned politically motivated book removals, but strongly suggested decisions based on educational suitability would be upheld, particularly where a regular system of review with standardized guidelines were in place.

Wallace v. Jaffree, 472 U.S. 38 (1985)

The Supreme Court upheld a First Amendment challenge to an Alabama law that required the school day to begin with a moment of silence for "meditation or voluntary prayer." The Court determined that the legislature clearly intended to return religion to the schools in violation of the Establishment Clause. The Court found the unambiguous legislative record indicated that "the statute had *no* secular purpose." By conveying the message that the moment of silence ought to be used for prayer, the schools were unconstitutionally sponsoring a religious exercise, thereby violating "the established principle that the Government must pursue a course of complete neutrality toward religion."

Bethel School District No. 403 v. Fraser, 478 U.S. ___ (1986)

A high school student was suspended for two days after making sexually suggestive remarks in a student-government nominating speech at a voluntary school assembly. The student's challenge of his suspension failed before the Supreme Court. It does not follow, the Court held, that "simply because the use of an offensive form of expression may not be prohibited to adults making what the speaker considers a political point, that the same latitude must be permitted to children in a public school." The Court went on to declare, "[t]he undoubted freedom to advocate unpopular and controversial views in schools and classrooms must be balanced against the society's countervailing interest in teaching students the boundaries of socially appropriate behavior."

San Diego Committee against Registration and the Draft (CARD) v. Governing Board of the Grossmont Union High School District, 790 F.2d 1471 (9th Cir. 1986)

A nonprofit group, known by the acronym, CARD, attempted to purchase advertising space for "information and counseling to male students regarding alternatives to military service" in five high school newspapers. A policy directive from the school district's superintendent instructed principals to reject the advertisement on the ground it would "contribute to the solicitation of illegal acts by the district's students." CARD brought a First Amendment challenge.

The Court of Appeals found that the school district's policies had created a limited public forum in the student newspapers. With respect to speech by nonstudents, the board's policy was to permit advertisements offering goods, services, or vocational opportunities to students. The school contended that its policy allowed only nonpolitical commercial speech. However, since the school permitted the newspapers to publish military recruitment advertising, which the court concluded was political or governmental and not economic, the CARD advertisement was "within the limited public forum the Board has created." To allow military recruitment advertising while denying advertising opposed to military service was to engage in impermissible viewpoint-based discrimination. In addition, the court determined that the advertisement's text failed to suggest the advocacy of illegal activity, and the Board's speculation about that result did not provide a reasonable basis for excluding the advertisement.

Fowler v. Board of Education of Lincoln County, Kentucky, 819 F.2d 657 (6th Cir. 1987)

A tenured high school teacher was discharged in July 1984 after she permitted students under her charge, ages 14 to 17, to view an R-rated movie, "Pink Floyd—The Wall," while she completed grade cards. In permitting the showing of the movie with which she was unfamiliar, the teacher was responding to a request from the students. She asked a student familiar with the film to edit out unsuitable portions by use of a file folder that covered only part of the screen. School officials charged that the movie promoted values that were immoral, antieducation, antifamily, antijudiciary, and antipolice, as well as was objectionable for its sexual content, vulgar language, and violence.

The Court of Appeals held "that conduct is protected by the First Amendment *only* when it is expressive or communicative in nature." Since the teacher had not seen the movie, the court reasoned that she could not have had the intent to convey a particular message and was not within her First Amendment rights. The teacher's discharge was thus upheld.

Bystrom v. Fridley High School Independent School District No. 14, 822 F.2d 747 (8th Cir. 1987)

Students brought suit challenging a school policy giving officials review and a right to prevent distribution on school premises of their "underground newspaper." The Court of Appeals held that prior restraints in the high school context are not *per se* unconstitutional and that government may regulate the distribution of written materials that fall within guidelines outlining what is "obscene to minors," libelous, pervasively indecent or vulgar, invading privacy, or advertising products or services not permitted to minors by law. In addition, schools may regulate such distributions to prevent a "substantial disruption of the proper and orderly operation and discipline of a school." The court upheld the school policy in this case except as it related to invasion of privacy or endangering the health or safety of another, since it would not result in tort liability to "the school or anyone else."

Smith v. Board of School Commissioners of Mobile County, 827 F.2d 684 (11th Cir. 1987)

Parents and other citizens in Mobile, Alabama, brought a lawsuit against the school board, alleging that the school system was teaching the tenets of an anti-religious religion called "secular humanism." The plaintiffs, all Christian Evangelicals, claimed that the teaching of this religion violated the First Amendment's Establishment Clause, which forbids government from promoting any or all religions. To remedy the alleged violation, the complainants asked that 44 different elementary through high school level textbooks be removed from the curriculum of the school district. After the plaintiffs won an initial victory against some of the textbooks in the federal district court, the U.S. Court of Appeals for the Eleventh Circuit reversed.

The court, avoiding the issue of whether "secular humanism" is a religion, held that as long as the school was motivated by a secular purpose, it didn't matter whether the curriculum and texts shared ideas held by one or more religious groups. The court found that the texts in question promoted important secular values, including tolerance, self-respect, and logical decision making. Thus, the use of the textbooks in dispute did not unconstitutionally advance a non-theistic religion, nor inhibit theistic religions.

Mozert v. Hawkins County Board of Education, 827 F.2d 1058 (6th Cir. 1987)

Parents and students representing seven families with children in grades one through eight brought this action challenging the mandatory use of certain reading textbooks on the grounds that the texts promoted values offensive to their religious beliefs and constituted a violation of the Constitution's guarantee of religious liberty.

The U.S. Court of Appeals for the Sixth Circuit rejected the plaintiff's claim, stating that a "requirement that classes, in the absence of a showing that this participation entailed affirmation or denial of a religious belief, or performance or non-performance of a religious exercise or practice, does not place an unconstitutional burden on the students' free exercise of religion." In so holding, the court found that the Constitution does not require school curricula to be revised substantially in order to accommodate religious views.

Edwards v. *Aguillard*, 55 U.S.L.W. 4861 (1987)

Louisiana had enacted a law, known as the Creationism Act, that prohibited the teaching of evolution unless accompanied by the balanced treatment of "creation science." The statute was challenged, and the Supreme Court found that it violated the First Amendment's Establishment Clause. Because the statute mandated the creation of curriculum guides on creationism and prohibited discrimination against believers of creationism, and did not do the same for evolution, the Court determined that "the legislature therefore sought to alter the science curriculum to reflect endorsement of a religious view that is antagonistic to the theory of evolution." Schools cannot endorse a particular religious viewpoint and "seek to employ the symbolic and financial support of government" to do so, according to the decision.

Hazelwood School District v. *Kuhlmeier*, 86–836, 484 U.S. 260 (1988)

After a school principal removed two pages containing articles, among others, on teenage pregnancy and the impact of divorce on students from a newspaper produced as part of a high school journalism class, the student staff filed suit claiming a violation of their First Amendment rights. The principal defended his action on the grounds that he was protecting the privacy of the pregnant students described, protecting younger students from inappropriate references to sexual activity and birth control, and protecting the school from a potential libel action.

The Supreme Court held that the principal acted reasonably and did not violate the students' First Amendment rights. A school need not tolerate student speech, the Court declared, "that is inconsistent with its 'basic educational mission,' even though the government could not censor similar speech outside the school." In addition, the Court found the newspaper was part of the regular journalism curriculum and subject to extensive control by a faculty member. The school, thus, did not create a public forum for the expression of ideas, but instead maintained the newspaper "as a supervised learning experience for journalism students." The Court concluded that "educators do not offend the First Amendment by exercising editorial control over the style and content of student speech in school-sponsored expressive activities so long as their actions are reasonably related to legitimate pedagogical concerns." The Court strongly suggested that supervised student activities that "may fairly be characterized as part of the school curriculum," including school-sponsored publications and theatrical productions, were subject to the authority of educators. The Court cautioned, however, that this authority does not justify an educator's attempt "to silence a student's personal expression that happens to occur on the school premises."

Virgil v. School Board of Columbia County, 862 F.2d 1517 (11th Cir. 1989)

After parental complaints, the Columbia County school board removed to locked storage a literature textbook containing excerpts from the classic Greek comedy *Lysistrata*, by Aristophanes, and *The Miller's Tale*, by the medieval English poet Geoffrey Chaucer. The board agreed with parents that the passages were characterized by "explicit sexuality and excessively vulgar language."

Although the judges felt compelled to "seriously question how young persons just below the age of majority can be harmed by these masterpieces of Western literature," the court upheld the school board's action. The court focused on the fact that these were materials used within the curriculum and thus bore the imprimatur of school approval. It then found that the reason for the removal—sexuality and vulgar language—was a legitimate pedagogical concern. The court also found the board action reasonable because the textbook, as well as other versions of the disputed selections, remained available in the school library.

A Selected, Annotated Bibliography on the First Amendment and Intellectual Freedom

These titles, published during more than a decade of considerable attention to freedom of expression and censorship, reflect the major issues of the debate—freedom of the press; school and library censorship; and regulation of pornography. Titles range from popular to scholarly, theoretical to practical, and include important audiovisual items produced during the period.

Adams, Thelma, ed. *Censorship and First Amendment Rights: A Primer.* Tarrytown, New York: American Booksellers Foundation for Free Expression, 1992.
> Case studies and resources for handling censorship, working with lawyers and lobbyists, etc., with an introduction by Anthony Lewis.

Berninghausen, David K. *Flight from Reason: Essays on Intellectual Freedom in the Academy, the Press and the Library.* Chicago: American Library Association, 1975.
> Essays about intellectual freedom with a focus on pressures to censor from the right and the left. Also includes the role of the American Library Association in defense of intellectual freedom.

Bosmajian, Haig. *Censorship, Libraries and the Law.* New York: Neal-Schuman, 1983.
> Reprints of court cases related to school library censorship.

Bryson, Joseph E., and Elizabeth W. Detty. *Legal Aspects of Censorship of Public School Library and Instructional Materials.* Charlottesville, Virginia: Michie, 1982.

Designed to alert educators to critical censorship areas and to help them develop policies and procedures to avoid judicial action and adverse public relations resulting from censorship.

Burress, Lee. *Battle of the Books: Literary Censorship in the Public Schools, 1950–1985.* Metuchen, New Jersey: Scarecrow Press, 1989.
Case studies, issues, and surveys on public school censorship.

Busha, Charles H. *An Intellectual Freedom Primer.* Littleton, Colorado: Libraries Unlimited, 1977.
Intellectual freedom in the 20th century, ranging from the performing arts and cinema to data systems and censorship research.

Censorship or Selection: Choosing Books for Public Schools. [Video recording] Chicago: American Library Association, Washington, D.C.: Association of American Publishers with Media and Society Seminars, 1982.
Explores censorship in three areas: the classroom, the library, and textbooks—specifically, creationism/evolution. Who should determine content and who can remove materials?

Davis, James E., Ed. *Dealing with Censorship.* Urbana, Illinois: National Council of Teachers of English, 1979.
Articles by well-known intellectual freedom advocates Jenkinson, Donelson, Shugert, and others discussing issues related to censorship in schools.

DelFaltore, Joan. *What Johnny Shouldn't Read: Textbook Censorship in America.* New Haven, Connecticut: Yale University Press, 1992.
An enlightening treatise on how pressure groups affect textbook publishing, influencing schools throughout the country. The stories behind recent lawsuits show how local controversies become national issues because of sophisticated pressure group tactics.

Demac, Donna. *Liberty Denied: The Current Rise of Censorship in America.* Second edition. Rutgers, New York: Rutgers University Press, 1990.
A look at the rising tide of censorship in American society.

Downs, Robert B., and Ralph E. McCoy. *First Freedom Today: Critical Issues Relating to Censorship and to Intellectual Freedom.* Chicago: American Library Association, 1984.
Collection of writings on First Amendment issues during the last 25 years.

Freedom in America: The Two-Century Record. [Filmstrip] Chicago: Office for Intellectual Freedom, American Library Association, 1977.
Visual overview of First Amendment freedoms in America.

Geller, Evelyn. *Forbidden Books in American Public Libraries, 1876–1939: A Study in Cultural Change.* Westport, Connecticut: Greenwood Press, 1984.

A social history and analysis of the approach of the profession of librarianship to censorship and freedom to read.

Hentoff, Nat. *The First Freedom: The Tumultuous History of Free Speech in America.* New York: Delacorte Press, 1980.
Historical review of the First Amendment.

Jenkinson, Edward B. *Censors in the Classroom: The Mind Benders.* Carbondale, Illinois: Southern Illinois University Press, 1979.
Discussion of current censorship activity in the schools by a scholar in the field.

Jenkinson, Edward B. *The Schoolbook Protest Movement: 40 Questions and Answers.* Bloomington, Indiana: Phi Delta Kappa Educational Foundation, 1986.
Questions and answers on the significant issues of the school book censorship movement, most challenged materials, policies and procedures.

Jones, Frances J. *Defusing Censorship: The Librarians' Guide to Handling Censorship Conflicts.* Phoenix, Arizona: Oryx Press, 1983.
Overview of recent court cases and discussion of legal issues related to censorship, with procedures and advice for librarians.

Lewis, Felice Flanery. *Literature, Obscenity and Law.* Carbondale, Illinois: Southern Illinois University Press, 1976.
Historical overview of judicial actions related to literary classics.

Lofton, John. *Press as Guardian of the First Amendment.* Columbia, South Carolina: University of South Carolina Press, 1980.
Two hundred years of press reaction to the First Amendment.

Malakoff, Eve H., and Mark S. Wisniewski, Eds. *First Amendment and the Schools.* Washington, D.C.: National School Boards Association, Council of School Attorneys, 1983.
First Amendment issues related to library books, textbooks, religion, and student publications from the point of view of school board attorneys. Includes George Lipp commenting on the Island Trees case.

Marsh, Dave. *50 Ways to Fight Censorship.* New York, New York: Thunder's Newsletter Press, 1991.
A pull no punches guide to fighting censorship wherever it may appear.

Moshman, David, Ed. *Children's Intellectual Rights* (New Directions for Child Development, No. 33). San Francisco, California: Jossey-Bass, Inc. 1986.
Six essays addressing the issue of whether and to what extent First Amendment guarantees apply to children and adolescents.

Newsletter on Intellectual Freedom. Chicago: Intellectual Freedom Committee, American Library Association.

Bimonthly journal providing essential news and features about intellectual freedom and censorship activity.

Noble, William. *Bookbanning in America: Who Bans Books?—And Why?* Middlebury, Vermont: Paul S. Eriksson, 1990.
Anecdotes, interviews, trial transcripts, and case histories show how and why bookbanning happens, beginning in 1650, through the recent and aging Salman Rushdie affair.

Oboler, Eli M., Ed. *Censorship and Education.* New York: H. W. Wilson, 1981.
Typical "reference shelf" reprints of significant articles about classroom and library censorship.

Oboler, Eli M. *Defending Intellectual Freedom.* Westport, Connecticut: Greenwood Press, 1980.
Collection of Oboler writings on censorship and intellectual freedom.

Office for Intellectual Freedom. American Library Association. *Censorship Litigation and the Schools: Proceedings of a Colloquium Held January 1981.* Chicago: American Library Association, 1983.
Edited transcript of a colloquium sponsored by American Civil Liberties Union, Association of American Publishers, American Library Association, and Freedom to Read Foundation.

Office for Intellectual Freedom. American Library Association. *Intellectual Freedom Manual.* Fourth Edition. Chicago and London: American Library Association, 1992.
Basic reference outlining official ALA policy relating to Intellectual Freedom including the Library Bill of Rights and interpretations. Essential information for all in the library community.

O'Neil, Robert M. *Classrooms in the Crossfire: The Rights of Students, Parents, Teachers, Administrators, Librarians and the Community.* Bloomington, Indiana: Indiana University Press, 1981.
"A major premise of the book is that more and better information . . . about conditions and hazards will better maintain the freedom which is a cornerstone of our educational system." (p. x, Preface).

Parker, Barbara, and Stefanie Weiss. *Protecting the Freedom to Learn: A Citizen's Guide.* Washington, D.C.: People for the American Way, 1983.
A practical guide for those who want to eliminate censorship from the public schools.

Robotham, John, and Gerald Shields. *Freedom of Access to Library Materials.* New York: Neal-Schuman, 1982.
Intellectual freedom issues in the 1980s, including pressure groups, access to nonprint materials, and isms.

Schexnaydre, Linda, Nancy Burns and Emporia State University School of Library and Information Management. *Censorship: A Guide for Successful Workshop Planning.* Phoenix, Arizona: Oryx Press, 1984.

Planning and conducting intellectual freedom workshops. Includes timelines, programs, and materials.

Speaker: *A Film about Freedom.* [Motion Picture] Chicago: Office for Intellectual Freedom, American Library Association, 1977.

Conflict arises when a controversial speaker is invited to a local high school. Illustrates reactions and pressures that occur when a censorship incident happens.

Stevens, John D. *Shaping the First Amendment: The Development of Free Expression.* Beverly Hills: Sage Publications, 1982.

Overview of shapers of the First Amendment—American history, wars, ideologies, editors, "protectors," and new technology.

Thomas, Cal. *Book Burning.* Westchester, Illinois: Crossway Books, Good News Publishers, 1983.

A speech at the American Library Association's 1982 annual conference expanded into a book. Moral Majority leader Thomas suggests that the modern censors are librarians who attempt to keep points of view different from their own from libraries.

Woods, L. B. *A Decade of Censorship in America: The Threat to Classrooms and Libraries, 1966–1975.* Metuchen, New Jersey: Scarecrow Press, 1979.

A study of 900 cases of censorship reported in the *Newsletter on Intellectual Freedom.*

Notes

Chapter 1

1. *Tinker v. Des Moines Independent Community School District*, 393 U.S. 503 (1969).
2. *Newsletter on Intellectual Freedom*, March 1987, p. 52.
3. *Epperson v. Arkansas*, 393 U.S. 97 (1968).
4. *Keyishian v. Board of Regents*, 385 U.S. 589 (1976).
5. *Board of Education, Island Trees v. Pico*, 102 U.S. 2799 (1982).
6. Mark G. Yudof, "The State as Editor or Censor: Book Selection and the Public Schools," in American Library Association, Office for Intellectual Freedom, *Censorship Litigation and the Schools: Proceedings of a Colloquium Held January 1981* (Chicago, 1983), pp. 50–51.
7. *Newsletter on Intellectual Freedom*, March 1987, p. 52.
8. Yudof, "State as Editor," p. 50.
9. Connecticut State Board of Education, "Free to Learn: A Policy on Academic Freedom and Public Education," Adopted September 9, 1981; Minnesota State Board of Education, "A Policy on the Freedom to Teach, to Learn, and to Express Ideas in the Public Schools," adopted March 12, 1985.
10. Robert M. O'Neil, "Current Social and Political Trends and Their Implications for Future Legislation," in ALA, *Censorship Litigation and the Schools*, p. 14.
11. *Tinker v. Des Moines Independent Community School District*, 393 U.S. 503 (1969).
12. American Association of University Professors, Commission on Academic Freedom and Pre-College Education, *Liberty and Learning in the Schools: Higher Education's Concerns* (Washington, D.C., 1986), p. 5.
13. O'Neil, "Current Trends," p. 13.
14. AAUP, *Liberty and Learning in the Schools*, p. 9.
15. Alexander Meiklejohn, "Teachers and Controversial Questions," reprinted in Cynthia Stokes Brown, ed., *Alexander Meiklejohn: Teacher of Freedom* (Berkeley, Calif., 1981), p. 214.
16. U.S. National Commission on Libraries and Information Science, *Censorship Activities in Public and Public School Libraries, 1975–1985* (Washington, D.C., March 1986).
17. People for the American Way, *Attacks on the Freedom to Learn, 1990–91* (Washington, D.C., 1991). *Newsletter on Intellectual Freedom*, November 1991, p. 189; November 1992, p. 179.

18. Association of American Publishers, American Library Association, Association for Supervision and Curriculum Development, *Limiting What Students Shall Read: Books and Other Learning Materials in Our Public Schools: How They Are Selected and How They Are Removed* (Washington, D.C., 1981). For a summary of the report's findings by its principal author, see Michelle Marder Kamhi, "Censorship vs. Selection—Choosing the Books Our Children Shall Read," *Educational Leadership*, December 1981, pp. 211–15.

19. Lee Burress, *Books Under Attack in the American School System, 1963–1985* (Urbana, Ill., 1985); *Summary Report of a Survey of Censorship Pressures on the American High School* (Urbana, Ill., 1983).

20. Dianne McAfee Hopkins, *Factors Influencing the Outcome of Challenges to Materials in Secondary School Libraries: Report of a National Study* (Madison, Wisconsin: School of Library and Information Studies, 1991). See also *Newsletter on Intellectual Freedom*, January 1992, p. 1.

21. Sissy Kegley and Gene Guerrero, *Censorship in the South: A Report of Four States, 1980–1985* (Atlanta, Georgia, 1986). See also *Newsletter on Intellectual Freedom*, March 1986, pp. 29, 56.

22. *Newsletter on Intellectual Freedom*, March 1990, p. 42; September 1990, p. 157–58.

23. *Newsletter on Intellectual Freedom*, November 1992, p. 179.

24. A. M. Scott, "Censorship in Virginia Public High School Libraries, 1979–82," MSLS dissertation, University of Virginia, 1982.

25. *Newsletter on Intellectual Freedom*, November 1987, p. 219.

26. *Attacks on the Freedom to Learn, 1990–91* (Washington, D.C., 1991), p. 4. *Newsletter on Intellectual Freedom*, November 1992, p. 179.

27. Fran McDonald, *A Report of a Survey on Censorship in Public Elementary and High School Libraries and Public Libraries in Minnesota* (Minneapolis, 1983). *Newsletter on Intellectual Freedom*, March 1992, p. 32.

28. A. McClure, *Censorship in Ohio: It Is Happening Here* (Delaware, Ohio, 1982).

29. *Newsletter on Intellectual Freedom*, July 1992, p. 103.

30. *Newsletter on Intellectual Freedom*, November 1989, p. 215; July 1990, p. 124.

31. *Attacks on the Freedom to Learn, 1990–91*, pp. 4–5.

32. *Newsletter on Intellectual Freedom*, March 1991, p. 36.

33. *Attacks on the Freedom to Learn, 1990–91*, p. 5.

34. *Newsletter on Intellectual Freedom*, July 1987, pp. 126–27.

35. John F. Wakefield, "Portrait of a Censor," *Newsletter on Intellectual Freedom*, March 1989, p. 33.

36. This section is adopted from American Library Association, Office for Intellectual Freedom, *Intellectual Freedom Manual*, 4th edition, (Chicago and London, 1992), pp. 235–36.

37. This is the conclusion of both the People for the American Way reports and the study by Professor Hopkins.

38. *Newsletter on Intellectual Freedom*, September 1990, p. 158; July 1991, p. 104.

39. *Limiting What Students Shall Read*, p. 23.

40. *Rocky Mountain News*, July 5, 1987, p. 6.

41. *Attacks on the Freedom to Learn, 1990–91*, p. 13.
42. Diane McAfee Hopkins, "Why School Book Challenges Succeed or Fail," *Newsletter on Intellectual Freedom*, January 1992, p. 1.
43. *Newsletter on Intellectual Freedom*, March 1986, p. 56.

Chapter 2

1. American Library Association, "Library Bill of Rights," in *Intellectual Freedom Manual*, 4th edition, (Chicago and London, 1992), p. 3.
2. June Berkley, Department of English, Ohio University, quoted in *Censorship or Selection: Choosing Books for Public Schools: Discussion Guide for a Videotape* (Washington D.C. and Chicago, 1982), p. 5.
3. Judy Blume, children's and young adult author, quoted ibid.
4. American Library Association, "Access to Resources and Services in the School Library Media Program: An Interpretation of the Library Bill of Rights" in *Intellectual Freedom Manual*, p. 86.
5. "Free Access to Libraries for Minors: An Interpretation of the Library Bill of Rights," in *Intellectual Freedom Manual*, p. 17.
6. *Newsletter on Intellectual Freedom*, March 1985, p. 33.
7. "Free Access to Libraries for Minors," *Intellectual Freedom Manual*, p. 16.
8. "Diversity in Collection Development: An Interpretation of the Library Bill of Rights," in *Intellectual Freedom Manual*, pp. 49–50.
9. Judge Ralph Winter, United States Court of Appeals, Second Circuit, quoted in *Censorship or Selection*, p. 5.
10. *Newsletter on Intellectual Freedom*, January 1991, p. 9; September 1991, p. 154; November 1991, p. 195.
11. *Newsletter on Intellectual Freedom*, July 1992, p. 117. For more on the controversy over *Impressions* see chapter 3 and *Newsletter on Intellectual Freedom*, January 1991, pp. 14, 15, 17, 29; March 1991, pp. 46–48; May 1991, 76, 91; July 1991, pp. 107, 109, 131–33; September 1991, pp. 178–79; November 1991, p. 197; January 1992, pp. 7, 9; March 1992, pp. 32, 45; September 1992, p. 163.
12. *Newsletter on Intellectual Freedom*, March 1992, p. 64.
13. *Virgil v. School Board of Columbia County,* 862 F.2d 1517 (11th Cir. 1989).
14. *Charleston Post and Courier*, January 17, 1993. For another incident involving DUSO as well as Pumsy, this time in Clay County, Florida, see *Newsletter on Intellectual Freedom*, November 1992, p. 186.
15. *Wisconsin v. Yoder*, 406 U.S. 205 (1972).
16. *Newsletter on Intellectual Freedom*, January 1987, p. 1; November 1987, p. 217.
17. *Tinker v. Des Moines Independent Community School District*, 393 U.S. 503 (1969). For a brief account of the *Tinker* case and of its initial application to high school journalism see Nat Hentoff, *The First Freedom: The Tumultuous History of Free Speech in America* (New York, 1980), pp. 1–22.
18. *Hazelwood School District v. Kuhlmeier*, 484 U.S. 260, 108 S.Ct. 562 (1988). For more on *Hazelwood* see chapter 6 and *Intellectual Freedom Manual*, pp.

186–92 and Student Press Law Center, *Law of the Student Press* (Washington, D.C., 1985, 1992), addendum, pp. 81–93.
19. *Captive Voices: The Report of the Commission of Inquiry into High School Journalism* (New York, 1974), p. 136.

Chapter 3

1. National Association of Secondary School Principals, *The Bulletin*, September 1961.
2. *Newsletter on Intellectual Freedom*, July 1991, p. 103; July 1992, p. 105.
3. Ibid., January 1993, p. 10
4. Ibid., March 1986, p. 40.
5. *Hampshire Gazette*, September 25, 1987, October 29, 1987; *Boston Globe*, November 8, 1987.
6. *Newsletter on Intellectual Freedom*, November 1992, p. 187; July 1992, p. 107, 124; January 1990, p. 32–33.
7. Ibid, March 1986, p. 42.
8. Ibid., July 1986, p. 115.
9. Ibid., March 1986, p. 40.
10. Ibid., May 1992, p. 81.
11. Ibid., May 1987, p. 85.
12. Ibid., p. 103.
13. Ibid., January 1993, p. 13; March 1987, p. 67.
14. Ibid., May 1987, p. 90; March 1992, p. 64; September 1992, p. 163.
15. Ibid., March 1992, p. 41; May 1987, p. 90.
16. Ibid., May 1992, p. 96.
17. Ibid., March 1987, p. 49.
18. Kenneth Bradford, "Report to the Virginia Board of Education on Changes in Works Contained in Secondary Literature Textbooks," *Newsletter on Intellectual Freedom*, May 1985, pp. 67, 93–95.
19. American Association of University Professors, Commission on Academic Freedom and Pre-College Education, *Liberty and Learning in the Schools: Higher Education's Concerns* (Washington, D.C., 1986), p. 11.
20. Norma Klein, "Some Thoughts on Censorship: An Author Symposium," *Top of the News*, Winter 1983, p. 140.
21. *Newsletter on Intellectual Freedom*, March 1987, p. 66.
22. Ibid., p. 67.
23. Ibid., January 1992, p. 5–6.
24. Ibid., November 1992, p. 182.
25. Ibid., March 1987, p. 52.
26. Ibid., September 1992, p. 141.
27. Ibid., July 1992, p. 112; May 1992, pp. 82–83.
28. Ibid., March 1987, p. 53.
29. Ibid., March 1992, p. 40.
30. Ibid., September 1991, pp. 173–74.
31. Ibid., September 1992, p. 138; May 1992, p. 80.

32. *Intellectual Freedom Manual*, p. 34.
33. William M. Bowen, Jr., *Globalism: America's Demise* (Shreveport, La., 1984), p. 15 as quoted in Edward Jenkinson, "New Age: Target of the Censor," *Newsletter on Intellectual Freedom*, November 1988, p. 189.
34. Texe Marrs, *Secrets of the New Age* (Westchester, Ill., 1988), p. 230 as quoted ibid, p. 220.
35. *Torcasco v. Watkins*, 367 U.S. 488 (1961).
36. *Newsletter on Intellectual Freedom*, May 1987, pp. 75, 104–7.
37. American Association of School Administrators, *Religion in the Public Schools* (Arlington, Va., 1986), p. 40.
38. *Newsletter on Intellectual Freedom*, January 1993, p. 9.
39. Ibid., July 1992, p. 108.
40. Ibid., May 1992, p. 78. Incidents in which children's Halloween books and "scary stories" anthologies have been challenged are numerous. Interested readers can find accounts of dozens of such instances from all parts of the country and all kinds of school districts in every issue of the *Newsletter on Intellectual Freedom* for 1991 and 1992.
41. Ibid., May 1992, pp. 80, 82.
42. Ibid., January 1993, p. 12.
43. Ibid., p. 18.
44. Ibid., November 1992, p. 186; January 1993, p. 11.
45. Ibid., January 1986, p. 21.
46. On *Impressions* see *Attacks on the Freedom to Learn, 1990–91*, pp. 8–9 and *Newsletter on Intellectual Freedom*, March 1991, pp. 46–48; July 1991, pp. 131–32; July 1992, p. 117.
47. *Newsletter on Intellectual Freedom*, July 1992, p. 117.
48. *Epperson v. Arkansas* 393 U.S. 97 (1968).
49. *Edwards v. Aguillard*, 55 U.S.L.W. 4861 (U.S. June 16, 1987)(No. 85–1513).
50. Patricia Lines, "Scientific Creationism in the Classroom: A Constitutional Dilemma," *Loyola Law Review*, XXVIII, 1982, reprinted in *NCRPE Bulletin*, Summer 1983, p. 36.
51. *Science and Creationism: A View from the National Academy of Sciences* (Washington, D.C., 1984), p. 7.
52. In March 1984, the Texas attorney general issued an advisory opinion that this rule violated the First and Fourteenth Amendments, and a month later the board voted to repeal it.
53. AAUP, *Liberty and Learning in the Schools*, p. 10.
54. *Newsletter on Intellectual Freedom*, January 1985, p. 38.
55. Ibid., September 1992, p. 140.
56. Ibid., March 1991, p. 44.

Chapter 4

1. Minnesota Civil Liberties Union, "What to Do about Censorship in the Public Schools," undated brochure.

2. *Board of Education, Island Trees Union Free School District* v. *Pico* 102 U.S. 2799 (1982).
3. The remainder of this chapter is principally adopted from material in American Library Association, Office for Intellectual Freedom, "Workbook for Selection Policy Writing" (mimeographed) and *Intellectual Freedom Manual*, 4th edition, (Chicago, 1992), pp. 207–14.
4. Here and elsewhere in this book discussion of student press rights is based principally on the booklet *Law of the Student Press*, published by the Student Press Law Center, Washington, D.C.

Chapter 5

1. Minnesota Civil Liberties Union, "What to Do about Censorship in the Public Schools," undated brochure.
2. Portions of this chapter are adopted from American Library Association, *Intellectual Freedom Manual*, 4th edition, (Chicago and London, 1992), pp. 215–22, 237–38, 254–56, 263–67.

Chapter 6

1. *West Virginia State Board of Education* v. *Barnette*, 319 U.S. 624 (1943).
2. Mark G. Yudof, "The State as Editor or Censor: Book Selection and the Public School," in American Library Association, Office for Intellectual Freedom, *Censorship Litigation and the Schools* (Chicago, 1983), p. 49.
3. *Hazelwood School District* v. *Kuhlmeier*, 56 U.S.L.W. 4082 (1988).
4. William D. North, "School Library Censorship and the Courts: Before Hazelwood," in American Library Association, *Intellectual Freedom Manual*, 4th edition, (Chicago and London, 1992), pp. 175–85.
5. Robert M. O'Neil, "Current Social and Political Trends and Their Implications for Future Litigation," in *Censorship Litigation and the Schools*, pp. 4–15.
6. Ibid., p. 4.
7. *Board of Education, Island Trees Union Free School District* v. *Pico*, 457 U.S. 853, 102 S. Ct. 2799, 73 L.Ed.2d. 435 (1982).
8. The remainder of this section is adopted from North, "School Censorship and the Courts: Before Hazelwood," pp. 177–80
9. *Presidents Council, District 25* v. *Community School Board No. 25*, 457 F.2d 289 (2nd Cir. 1972), 409 U.S. 998 (1972).
10. *Minarcini* v. *Strongsville City School District*, 541 F.2d 577 (6th Cir. 1976).
11. *Right to Read Defense Committee* v. *School Committee of the City of Chelsea*, 454 F. Supp. 703 (D. Mass. 1978); *Salvail* v. *Nashua Board of Education*, 469 F. Supp. 1269 (1979).
12. *Zykan* v. *Warsaw Community School Corporation and Warsaw School Board of Trustees*, 631 F.2d 1300 (7th Cir. 1980).
13. *Bicknell* v. *Vergennes Union High School Board*, 475 F. Supp. 615 (D. Vt. 1979), 638 F.2d 438 (2d Cir. 1980); *Pico* v. *Board of Education, Island Trees*, 474 F. Supp. 387 (E.D.N.Y. 1979), 638 F.2d 404 (2d Cir. 1980).

14. North, "School Library Censorship and the Courts: Before Hazelwood," p. 179.
15. *Newsletter on Intellectual Freedom,* July 1992, p. 117; January 1993, p. 18.
16. American Association of School Administrators, *Religion in the Public Schools* (Arlington, Va., 1986). Available from AASA, 1801 N. Moore St., Arlington, VA 22209.
17. *Wallace v. Jaffree,* 105 S.Ct. 2479, concurring opinion (1985).
18. *Walz v. Tax Commission,* 397 U.S. 664, 694 (1970).
19. Thayer S. Warshaw, *Religion, Education and the Supreme Court* (Nashville, 1979), unpublished revisions, p. 11 as cited in AASA, *Religion in the Public Schools,* p. 11.
20. *Edwards v. Aguillard,* 55 U.S.L.W. 4861 (U.S. June 16, 1987) (No. 85–1513).
21. *Everson v. Board of Education,* 330 U.S. 1, (1947).
22. *Lemon v. Kurtzman,* 403 U.S. 602 (1971).
23. *Newsletter on Intellectual Freedom,* September 1992, pp. 151–55, 175.
24. *Epperson v. Arkansas,* 393 U.S. 97 (1968).
25. Ibid.
26. *Edwards v. Aguillard.*
27. Ibid.
28. *Tinker v. Des Moines Independent Community School District,* 393 U.S. 503 (1969).
29. Student Press Law Center, *Law of the Student Press* (Washington, 1985, 1992), available from SPLC, Suite 300, 800 18th St., NW, Washington, DC 20006. The 1992 printing of this pamphlet includes an extensive addendum on student press rights after the U.S. Supreme Court's 1988 *Hazelwood* decision. The following account of student press law is also based in part on "Freedom of the Press for Students," an unpublished April 1987 memorandum prepared by Mark Goodman, executive director of SPLC.
30. *Hazelwood School District v. Kuhlmeier,* 484 U.S. 260, 108 S.Ct. 562, 98 L.Ed.2d 592 (1988).
31. *Antonelli v. Hammond,* 308 F. Supp. 1329 (D.Mass, 1970). See also *Reineke v. Cobb County School District,* 484 F. Supp. 1252 (N.D. Ga. 1980); *Gambino v. Fairfax County School Board,* 429 F. Supp. 731 (E.D. Va.), *aff'd per curiam,* 564 F. 2d 157 (4th Cir. 1977); *Bayer v. Kinzler,* 383 F. Supp. 1164 (E.D.N.Y.), *aff'd without opinion,* 515 F. 2d 504 (2d Cir. 1975); *Koppell v. Levine,* 347 F. Supp. 456 (E.D.N.Y. 1972); *Zucker v. Panitz,* 299 F. Supp. 102 (S.D.N.Y. 1969).
32. *Hazelwood School District v. Kuhlmeier,* 484 U.S. 260 (1988).
33. Ibid.
34. Ibid.
35. Ibid. (Brennan, J., dissenting)
36. *Baughman v. Freienmuth,* 478 F.2d 1345 (1973); *Nitzberg v. Parks,* 525 F.2d 378 (4th Cir. 1975); *Shanley v. Northeast Independent School District,* 462 F.2d 960 (5th Cir. 1972); *Eisner v. Stamford Board of Education,* 440 F.2d 803 (2d Cir. 1971); *Sword v. Fox,* 446 F.2d 1091, 1097 (4th Cir.), *cert. denied,* 404 U.S. 994 (1971). But, for a more restrictive decision governing distribution of non-sponsored literature see *Bystrom v. Fridley High School,* _____, 8th Cir., Slip Op. 86–5140 (1987).
37. *Newsletter on Intellectual Freedom,* March 1988, p. 48.

38. *Tinker* v. *Des Moines Independent Community School District,* 393 U.S. 503 (1969).
39. Ibid.
40. *Jacobs* v. *Board of School Commissioners,* 490 F.2d 601 (7th Cir. 1973), *vacated as moot,* 420 U.S. 128 (1975). *Sullivan* v. *Houston Independent School District,* 475 F.2d 1071 (5th Cir.), *cert. denied,* 414 U.S. 1032 (1973) ("High Skool [sic] is Fucked" phrase not censorable); *Kopell* v. *Levine,* 347 F. Supp. 456 (E.D.N.Y. 1972). On Supreme Court definitions of "obscene as to minors" see: *Miller* v. *California,* 413 U.S. 15 (1973); *Ginsberg* v. *New York,* 390 U.S. 629 (1968).
41. *Scoville* v. *Board of Education,* 286 F. Supp. 988 (N.D. Ill. 1968), *rev'd,* 425 F.2d 10 (7th Cir.), *cert. denied,* 400 U.S. 826 (1970).
42. *New York Times* v. *Sullivan,* 376 U.S. 254 (1964); *Winter* v. *Northern Tier Publishing Co.,* 4 Med. L. Rptr. 1348 (N.Y.S.Ct. Westchester Co. 1978); *Milkovich* v. *News-Herald,* 11 Med. L. Rptr. 1598 (Ohio 1984).
43. This section is based on Robert S. Peck, "School Library Censorship and the Courts: After Hazelwood," in American Library Association *Intellectual Freedom Manual,* 4th edition, (Chicago and London, 1992), pp. 186–92.
44. *Virgil* v. *School Board of Columbia County,* 862 F.2d 1517 (11th Cir. 1989).
45. *Romano* v. *Harrington,* 725 F.Supp. 687 (D.N.Y. 1989).

Chapter 7

1. Michelle Marder Kamhi, "Censorship vs. Selection—Choosing the Books Our Children Shall Read," *Educational Leadership,* December 1981, p. 211.

Chapter 8

1. *Shelton* v. *Tucker,* 364 U.S. 479 (1960).
2. Nat Hentoff, *The First Freedom: The Tumultuous History of Free Speech in America* (New York, 1980).
3. June Berkley, "Teach the Parents Well: An Anti-Censorship Experiment in Adult Education," in *Dealing with Censorship,* ed. James E. Davis (Urbana, Ill.: NCTE, 1979).
4. Dorothy M. Broderick, "Censorship: A Family Affair?" *Top of the News,* Spring 1979, p. 231.
5. Sidney J. Hook, 1984 Jefferson Lecture in the Humanities (Washington, D.C.) as quoted in AAUP, *Liberty and Learning in the Schools,* p. 3a.

Henry Reichman has been associate editor and principal writer of the American Library Association's bimonthly *Newsletter on Intellectual Freedom* since 1982, having served previously as assistant editor in 1980–81, when he was also assistant director of ALA's Office for Intellectual Freedom. Dr. Reichman is a 1969 graduate of Columbia University and earned the Ph.D. in history from the University of California, Berkeley, in 1977. He has taught at several universities and is associate professor of history at California State University, Hayward. A specialist in Russian history, he is the author of an historical monograph and numerous scholarly articles and reviews.